NATURE NOTES
OCEAN VOYAGERS

BEING PERSONAL OBSERVATIONS UPON LIFE IN
"THE VASTY DEEP," AND FISHES, BIRDS, AND
BEASTS SEEN FROM A SHIP'S DECK; WITH
POPULAR CHAPTERS ON WEATHER, WAVES, AND
LEGENDARY LORE

BY

CAPTAIN ALFRED CARPENTER
R.N., D.S.O.

AND

CAPTAIN D. WILSON-BARKER
R.N.R.

"I can call spirits from the Vasty Deep"
GLENDOWER
In SHAKESPEARE's *King Henry IV*

With 139 Illustrations, including Map of the World

LONDON
CHARLES GRIFFIN & COMPANY LIMITED
PHILADELPHIA: J. B. LIPPINCOTT CO.
1915

H.M.S. "Challenger" at St. Paul's Rocks, Mid-Atlantic

PREFACE

THE authors of this book believe that no published work gives the amateur a comprehensive survey of the life, conditions, and phenomena occurring in the great ocean depths. Although considerable interest is taken in winds, tides, and surface disturbances by the average sailor, yachtsman and passenger, few concern themselves about the inhabitants of the waters on which they sail.

While this book was being prepared for publication, the *Challenger* Society brought out "The Science of the Sea," Sir John Murray and Dr. Johan Hjort together wrote "The Depths of the Ocean," and Sir John Murray also published "The Ocean." All these books are excellent and are most useful to those who wish to do some work for science, and who have already some elementary knowledge of the ocean and of the plants and animals living therein.

"Nature Notes for Ocean Voyagers" has not been written for such students, but for the many voyagers who feel a need for information on their unfamiliar surroundings at sea: it deals with Marine Natural History in its broadest and most old-fashioned sense. Facts only are affirmed and no special scientific order is adhered to. The book is mainly intended as a reference for amateurs. The authors have been in intimate association with the life about which they write. They describe just the general conditions of the sea; its circulation and temperature; the methods by which the ocean depths have been explored, and the life existing there ascertained. Other subjects dealt with are the Mammals and methods of "fishing" for whales; Birds and Reptiles, including notes on flight and migration; Fishes, with a particular note on the "flight" of the flying-fish, and the wonderful cuttle-fish; Plant Life and Seaweeds; Corals and Coral Reefs; life found at the surface and in ocean deposits. Chapter IX treats of the beautiful phenomena of Phosphorescence; mythical Sea Monsters; Weather and Waves. Old sea customs are also described, which, though apart from the foregoing subjects, are of interest to all lovers of ships and sailors. The charts illustrating Meteorological matter are constructed on the Flamsteed projection and were used to illustrate the presidential address given to the Royal Meteorological Society by Captain Wilson-Barker in 1904. The advantage of this system, which was devised by Flamsteed in 1700, is that all areas are shown truly, a valuable factor in meteorological work.

Captain Alfred Carpenter, R.N., D.S.O., was a lieutenant on board H.M.S. *Challenger* during her renowned scientific cruise round the world, and subsequently, as a naval surveyor, he had opportunities of deep-sea work in vessels under his command.

His collaborator, Captain David Wilson-Barker, R.N.R., served afloat for twenty years, of which ten were spent in sailing ships navigating in southern latitudes; he had also the valuable experience of deep-sea telegraph cable work. In continued pursuit of ocean research work, he has had the help through correspondence, of many officers of the Royal Navy and Mercantile Marine who were under him as cadets on the training-ship *Worcester*, which he has commanded for the past twenty-two years.

In the chapters on the physical properties of the ocean, authorities have been quoted, sometimes verbatim, but the use of inverted commas has been omitted. For such quotations the authors are particularly indebted to:

Moseley's "Notes by a Naturalist on the *Challenger*"; the Prince of Monaco's "Deep Sea Reports"; "The Science of the Sea," by the *Challenger* Society; "The Ocean," by Sir

John Murray ; "The Depths of the Ocean," by Sir John Murray and Dr. Johan Hjort ; and others mentioned in the text.

A few scientific terms have been used for the sake of brevity : they are fully explained in the Glossary.

The authors are greatly indebted to the Trustees of the British Museum (Nat. Hist.), the late Sir John Murray, Mr. James Chumley of the *Challenger* Office, Professor W. J. Sollas, C. Griffin & Co., T. Fisher Unwin, Mr. R. C. Mossman, Lieut.-Commander Cromie, R.N., Mr. Kirk, La Société D'Oceanographie du Golfe de Gasgogne, the Shipping World Ltd., and the Royal Meteorological Society, for many of the illustrations.

A. C.

D. W.-B.

London. 1915.

CONTENTS

xi

ILLUSTRATIONS

NATURE NOTES FOR OCEAN VOYAGERS

CHAPTER I

THE OCEAN

Depth. There is something about the word ocean that conveys a special charm to an Englishman. It brings to mind a great battlefield of chivalrous deeds ; it recalls many a brave man putting out into the unknown ; it enters into all our songs, our romances, and our history ; it is at once the Englishman's best bulwark and the grave of many of his greatest heroes. He clings to it as to a friend, and he rejoices in its might.

Nowadays there are few that have not sailed upon it, a still less few that have not seen it ; but we venture to think that there are very few who know much more about it than that it is salt, and that it is generally rough when they are on it.

In the earlier days of navigation its vastness gave rise to much superstition, and the old charts were embellished with drawings of sea monsters, submarine volcanoes, whirlpools, and destructive waterspouts. The mariner truly put to sea with his heart in his mouth, and the great pioneers of discovery, such as Columbus, Magellan, and Cook, had imaginary foes to contend with greater than any that really existed. The Maelstrom of the North Sea only died a natural death in the middle of the eighteenth century, and it is a question whether the belief in destructive waterspouts is yet extinct. In those early days the ocean was looked upon as the great barrier between nations, but now it forms the principal means of communication, affording a ready-made track almost as good as a railway line.

1   A

We do not propose in this book to describe its surface humours and pulsations which depend on the wooing of its fierce lover the wind, nor do we intend to touch upon the various forms of vessel that sail over it, nor upon the light-houses, buoys, and beacons that assist navigation.

Our desire is to put together in a popular form what is known of the extent and depth of the ocean; its temperatures and circulation, on which our climate so much depends; its extraordinary pressure by reason of its great bulk; some account of its inhabitants—not those usually seen laid out in our fish shops, but of the millions that are not so seen.

Then we shall describe the birds likely to be seen on a long voyage and give a pretty full description of the formation and life of a coral reef. Of course we can only touch lightly on such a large subject as Marine Zoology, and we shall do so more to interest the reader in processes that are going on in this great watery underworld than to give correct scientific descriptions of their structures.

That there is a floor to the ocean formed almost entirely of the remains of creatures which once lived at all depths is comparatively new knowledge not a century old, and the wonder of this has not perhaps been sufficiently put forward before.

The phenomena of phosphorescence, which plays a large part in ocean life, will also be described.

In 1872 the Royal Society induced the Admiralty to commission a man-of-war for the special purpose of investigating the depths; of rectifying open ocean charts in regard to numerous reported dangers; of making notes on meteorology and on marine currents; of visiting out-of-the-way islands to examine their fauna and flora, and particularly for taking notes of rapidly decaying races.

H.M.S. *Challenger*, a sloop of 2300 tons, was selected, a trained scientific staff was added to the usual complement of officers and men, and the ship spent three and a half years following out a definite cruise round the world, during which she covered 68,350 miles. The writer served as a young lieutenant on board for the last half of the cruise, and subsequently held appointments in command of surveying and exploring vessels for many years.

The publicity given to the purposes of the *Challenger* expedition created an emulative spirit among other nations; hence the United States and Germany followed suit almost immediately. One or two other nations then took up the research. Sir George Nares' Arctic expedition started before the return of the *Challenger*. Peary's work north of Greenland, and Nansen's great drift in the *Fram* across the Polar Sea, developed ocean research in new fields and led to attention being directed to the only unexplored region left, viz. the Antarctic continent.

Whilst England through Scott and Shackleton took the leading part in commencing to chart the Antarctic continent, many other nations have contributed to ocean research in southern latitudes.

Thus in the last forty years man has for the first time in history set himself to thoroughly explore the globe he lives on. That the ocean has received good attention is proved by the fact that up to 1912 about 6000 soundings have been made in depths greater than 1000 fathoms. Of these, 491 were in depths greater than 3000, and 46 in depths greater than 4000 fathoms.

The *Challenger* took about 375 deep soundings, and she used up 60 miles of sounding line.

A glance at a globe will show us that the extent of ocean surface is nearly three times that of the land; and it has been calculated that if the sea beds were emptied it would take thirteen times the present amount of dry land, that is to say land above sea level, to fill them. If the surface of the earth could be levelled so as to make a smooth circumference it follows that the ocean would surround it entirely as an envelope. It may not be realized that in such case the depth of the watery envelope would be nearly 10,000 feet. Possibly it was so at first, and that the heated waters hid all beneath. Then, as the water and crust of the earth cooled, contortions occurred due to shrinkage and the crust was pushed into crests and valleys like the wrinkles in the skin of a dried apple. The crests came above the waters which occupied the hollows.

Chemical salts, products of the cooling vapours, covered the surface and were washed down to the oceans by the rain, leaving the land surface to decay and form soil for organic growth. The sea became permanently salt, and charged with chemicals capable of dissolving all the impurities poured into it from the decay of organic matter.

From illustrations of relative depths and heights in text-books we are apt to get a false idea of the inequalities of the earth's surface. As a matter of fact, the surface of the globe is as smooth in proportion as the surface of a lemon, for if you conceive a globe 40 feet in diameter as representing the earth, the greatest height and the greatest depth would only be represented by an elevation or a depression of one third of an inch. Notwithstanding this, the heights and depths are relatively very considerable to us and appeal greatly to the imagination.

In the early centuries of the world's birth changes of surface must have been considerable, owing to contortion by shrinkage and to volcanic action, but it is not considered that the main outlines of oceans and continents have changed since Palæozoic times, although the presence of marine deposits shows that there have been periods of subsidence and re-elevation. The sea has by wear and tear, of course, made distinct inroads on the continents, and there is generally a shelf of comparatively shallow water, 80 to 100 fathoms, showing the denudation caused by wave action since the continents were formed.

On a bathymetrical chart one sees at a glance the possible changes that have occurred, such as the separation of Great Britain from Denmark, Holland and France by a slight sinking of the land level. Such probable changes are of great interest to students of natural history, for they account for similarity of fauna and flora in countries now separated. The size of a dividing sea is no indication of its depths, and it was not until deep sea sounding became common that bathymetrical charts could be drawn, and light thrown on ancient migration. To this day there are many problems that cannot be solved except by supposing land connexions over what are now the great ocean beds, and we shall not attempt to put forward any hypotheses.

Just as water in a glass is seen to be slightly drawn up where it is in contact with the glass, so the surface of the ocean is probably slightly raised by the proximity of land ridges.

The surface to us seems to be level, the fall toward mid-ocean being only about one foot in fourteen miles, but it is calculated that the surface of the water in mid-Pacific is some 350 feet nearer the centre of the earth than that on the borders of the continents.

The average height of land over the globe is 2200 feet, or 366 fathoms. The average depth of the sea is 2000 fathoms.

The depth of the ocean has ever had a great fascination over the mind of man, and the same thing occurs with lakes and mountain tarns, the local opinion generally being that they are " bottomless," whatever that may mean. During the *Challenger* cruise many mountain tarns were explored and soundings taken from an improvised raft.

Before steam came in to enable the mariner to keep his ship over one spot it was quite impossible to take an accurate sounding over 100 fathoms. The *Challenger* had moderate steam power, but was not fitted with the excellent sounding engines and wire line of the present day. She used Italian hemp, which, as it carried air down in its interstices, went slower and slower and marked the great depths badly. At our deepest sounding, which fell to the lot of the writer to take, and which was the first depth over 4000 fathoms till then recorded, we obtained 4475 fathoms, or 26,850 feet, near Guam Island in the Ladrones. The line took about an hour to run out, although we had four hundredweight on the end, and about two hours to reel in.   Several years later the writer with a Lucas wire machine took a sounding in 1600 fathoms, reeled in the wire again, and went ahead, all in forty minutes.

The weights on the hemp line were so heavy that they were slipped each time and left at the bottom, and it is possible that in future geological ages they will be recorded as meteorites that have come from some other planet !

The greatest depths that English ships have since obtained are 5022 fathoms south of the Friendly Islands, and 5155 fathoms east of the Kermadec Islands, which lie north-east of New Zealand.   Early in 1900 a United States vessel sounded round where the *Challenger* obtained 4475 fathoms, and obtained not far from it 5269 fathoms, which held the record until the German ship *Planet* in 1912 obtained 5348 fathoms off Mindanao, one of the Philippine Islands, in the same part of the Pacific.   This is just over 6 land miles or 32,088 feet, half a mile deeper than Mt. Everest is high.   The average depth of the Atlantic and of the Pacific is about $2\frac{3}{4}$ miles ; that of the Indian and Antarctic oceans about $2\frac{1}{3}$ miles ; the Mediterranean about $1\frac{1}{4}$ miles ; and the Arctic ocean, over a large section, 2 miles.   The latter is an enclosed sea, for both the Atlantic and Pacific are nearly shut off from it in Lat. 60° N. On the whole the tropical seas are the deepest.   Curiously enough, deep water is often found near continents.

We have already referred to the mistaken idea of the shape of the ocean beds that may be gathered from illustrations in text-books.   Owing to causes that will be described in Chapter VIII, gradients in deep water are very gentle, and the only abrupt slopes occur in quite shallow water.   From Sierra Leone to the West Indies the distance is 2700 miles, and the deep sounding of 3289 fathoms, near the middle of the line, gives a slope of only one in 360, which is practically level.

The actual operation of sounding is a difficult one even under steam.   There is generally a surface current overlying the still water below, the wind and waves tend to throw the

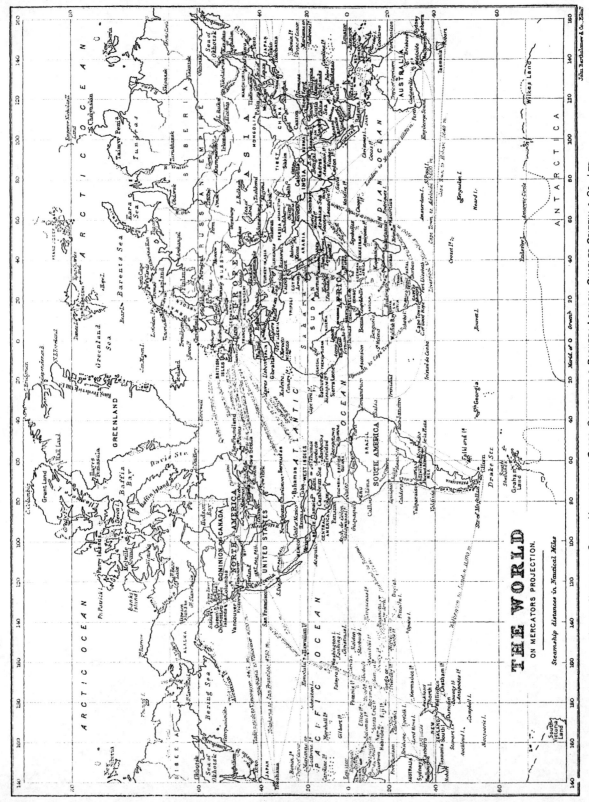

THE WORLD

ON MERCATORS PROJECTION.

Steamship distances in Nautical Miles.

NATURE NOTES FOR OCEAN VOYAGERS BY CAPTS. CARPENTER & BARKER: LONDON, CHARLES GRIFFIN & CO., LTD.

vessel out of position, the wire or line must be kept from getting under the ship or from fouling the screw. As many investigations require some action to take place when the instrument is deep down, such as the exposure of a photographic plate, the starting of a current meter, or the reversal of a thermometer, the desired effect is brought about by sending small weights, "messengers," down the line. These release or close catches as required on the submerged instrument.

A. C.

Temperature and Circulation. Although the temperature of the surface waters had been noted by mariners for many years and reduced by Maury and others to some order and connexion with ocean currents, but little reliable research had been carried out below the surface before the work of the *Lightning* and *Porcupine* in 1868–69. The temperatures taken all over the world during the *Challenger* cruise show that there is generally a rapid loss of heat from the surface down to 300 fathoms, then a lessening rate of fall down to 1200 fathoms, and then a fairly constant low temperature to the bottom. Surface currents seldom descend below 300 fathoms. Below 1200 there is an immense stratum of very cold water, ranging between 32° and 40°—the freezing-point of salt water being 28° Fahr. or −2° C.

Just as in our atmospheric ocean there is a complicated circulation of air brought about partly by the presence or the absence of the sun's heat, and partly by the earth's rotation, so in the watery ocean the same thing occurs.

The steady heat of the tropics warms the surface waters in low latitudes, the absence of the sun in the north and south reduces the polar waters to freezing temperatures.

Sea water increases in density as it cools down to 25° Fahr.; hence the colder and heavier water lies in a belt at the bottom. If we take a trough of water, warm one end and cool the other, the water will begin to circulate in the trough. That portion that is being warmed expands, comes to the surface as it becomes lighter, and necessarily spreads toward the cooler end. The water at the cold end, becoming heavy, sinks and travels toward the warm end to take the place of the rising water. In the N. and S. Atlantic Oceans and similarly in the Pacific we have practically two such troughs placed with their warm ends abutting on the equator, their cold ends in polar regions. An immense slow circulation takes place, which is effected by the rotation of the earth and by prevailing winds blowing continuously over large areas.

Owing to the rotation of the earth, a point on the equator is travelling eastward at nearly 1000 miles an hour. A point in Lat. 60° is only travelling eastward at half that speed owing to the smaller circumference of the earth in that latitude. Just as in stepping out of a moving vehicle you are thrown forward owing to the initial velocity you have acquired from the vehicle and not yet lost, so a body moving from the equator towards the poles is thrown to the eastward by reason of its initial velocity exceeding that of the latitude into which it is moving. A bullet fired in this country from south to north will at a distance of 1000 yards strike quite a measurable distance to the east of the point aimed at. Further, it can be shown that a body moving freely in the northern hemisphere in any direction will be deflected to the right owing to the earth's rotation ; and in the southern hemisphere to the left.

We therefore not only get a vast circulation between tropic and temperate regions owing to differences of temperature, but we get changes in the circulation owing to differences in speed of rotation. Add to these the surface circulation set up by long-continued action of the prevailing winds, and we get a good deal of movement. (Fig. 1.)

Differences of density and salinity also lead to vertical circulation. Where large amounts of fresh water enter the ocean, as in the Atlantic, or where there is prolonged evaporation owing to the sun's heat, there is necessarily a decrease or increase respectively of salinity. The cooling of the surface layers at night, and during winter in temperate regions, causes the salter

Fig. 1. In the Indian Ocean the currents are subject to change in the northern part with the monsoon changes. ∿→ N. winter, ∼→ N. summer :

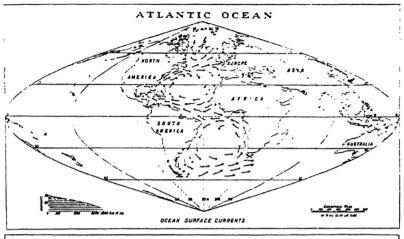

ATLANTIC OCEAN

OCEAN SURFACE CURRENTS

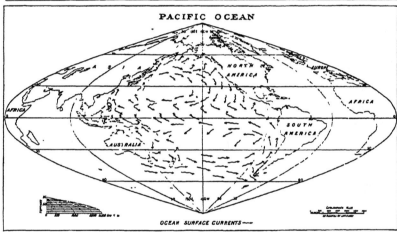

PACIFIC OCEAN

OCEAN SURFACE CURRENTS

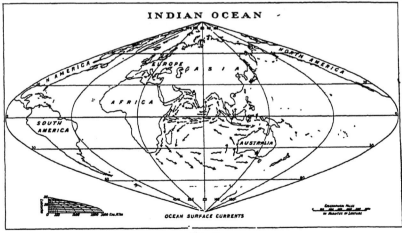

INDIAN OCEAN

OCEAN SURFACE CURRENTS

Fig. 1.

waters of the surface to sink through the underlying layers carrying with them warmth and atmospheric gases to the greater depths.

It is thought that the warm surface waters begin to sink in Lat. 50°, particularly so in the great southern oceans.

Temperatures are on the whole very regular at any one given spot throughout the year. The mean daily range of surface temperature at any one place on the open sea is under one degree. At a depth of 50 fathoms no greater annual range than two degrees has been found. At that depth the highest temperature will occur several months after the highest surface temperature has occurred. There is no evidence of any annual variation of temperature at any one spot in the ocean at a depth of 100 fathoms. But owing to the greater vertical circulation in one part of the ocean than in another, the temperature at 100 fathoms in one place may be as much as 42° higher than at another, and at 500 fathoms may vary as much as 20°. At 1500 fathoms no greater difference than 8° has been found.

There are over the globe many instances of seas, such as the Caribbean Sea, which are basins enclosed by a rim of comparatively shallow water. If the temperature was due merely to depth we should find low readings at the bottom of the basins. It is found, however, that the bottom temperature is always the same as that on the confining rim, and this shows that circulation is going on. When the abyssal cold water is forced up over the ridge it becomes warmed to a temperature due to the depth of the ridge, and carries that temperature down with it to the bottom of the basin.

Prolonged barometric pressure may also cause movement, but there is no doubt that the principal causes of ocean currents, at and near the surface, are the prevailing winds which depend on large barometrical weather systems (*see* Chapter XI).

The Gulf Stream is a movement started by the continual easterly winds blowing across the Atlantic in the northern tropics. The rotation of the earth and the configuration of the ocean basin gradually deflect this to the right until it forms an immense circular movement in the North Atlantic, carrying a warm body of air to our shores. The capacity of water for heat is very great, so that a comparatively small body of warm water will by losing its heat, warm an enormous bulk of air. Part of the north-going water cools and sinks again in Lat. 50° N., and no doubt joins the bottom stratum. One effect of the Gulf Stream is to heap up the water in the Gulf of Mexico, where it is considered to be forty inches above the level of the sea off New York.

As the prevailing wind blows off shore at Cape Verd in Africa, the warmest surface waters are blown away and there is an upwelling of cold. In polar seas, owing to the melting of the ice the cold water sometimes overlies the warmer, but as a general rule there is a steadily decreasing temperature to the bottom. The changes in mid-Atlantic are somewhat as follows :

At surface		81° Fahr.
10 fathoms		78·8° ,,
20 ,,		75·2° ,,
30 ,,		69·8° ,,
40 ,,		66·2° ,,
50 ,,		64·5° ,,
60 ,,		62·5° ,,
80 ,,		59·0° ,,
100 ,,		55·5° ,,
120 ,,		54·0° ,,
150 ,,		52·0° ,,
200 ,,		48·0° ,,
300 ,,		42·2° ,,
400 ,,		40·5° ,,
500 ,,		39·5° ,,
600 ,,		39·2° ,,
800 ,,		38·5° ,,
1000 ,,		38·0° ,,
1500 ,,		36·4° ,,
2000 ,,		35·6° ,,
3000 ,,		34·0° ,,

When a warm current meets a colder one, such as the meeting between the Gulf Stream and the Labrador current, the colder one sinks and passes under the warmer, and there is some overlapping of boundaries. When this occurs there is often great destruction of life unfitted to withstand the change, and ships in such localities have reported passing through many miles of dead fish.

At the Straits of Gibraltar, where there is a shelf of only 175 fathoms depth, the surface water down to about 75 fathoms is always flowing into the Mediterranean. Below that depth it flows slowly out.

Sea water contains oxygen, nitrogen, carbonic acid, and argon, the proportions varying. With increasing depth the carbonic acid increases and the oxygen decreases. Analyses of deep-sea water show the presence of absorbed oxygen everywhere which has been taken down from the surface by vertical currents, or by dust. But for this we should find no life in the greater depths. Marine animals require oxygen for respiration and they consume some of that contained in the water, thus producing carbonic acid. The minute plant life called diatoms which almost fill some seas, absorb a great deal of carbonic acid and produce oxygen. As the plant life (Plankton algæ) lives near the surface to get the light, oxygen is chiefly produced in the upper layers.

The average salinity of sea water is thirty-five parts of salts per thousand of water, and the ratio of the various salts is practically constant, chloride of sodium forming more than three-fourths of the solids.

Owing to the difference of temperature at different depths the range of zoological life is not confined to certain latitudes as it is on land. The aquatic traveller can seek his own climate without going very far. It has been found that not only a whole world of fishes, molluscs, medusæ, cephalopods and crustaceans, come to the surface at night and return before day to a depth of some hundreds of fathoms, but also that the larvæ of crustaceans and of shell fish, which form such a large pro-

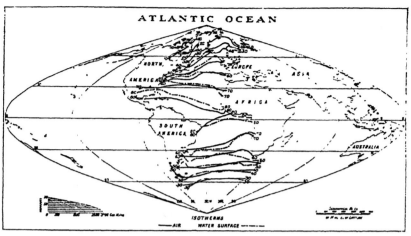

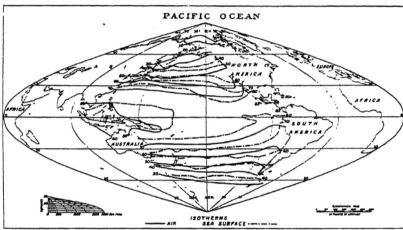

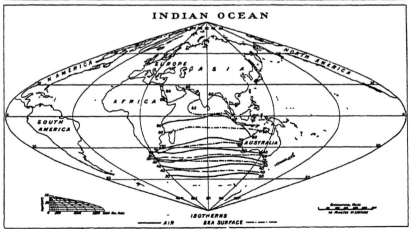

FIG 2.

portion of a surface catch (*see* Chapter VIII), go through a diurnal migration, rising at night and sinking by day.

It would be convenient in the British Isles if we too could in a few moments transport ourselves into a much warmer climate.   A. C.

Pressure.   That water is very heavy is not generally realized. Before the present system of a water-supply to tanks in the roof, when every can of water had to be carried up three or four stories, or hauled up from a well, it was better understood. A cubic foot of sea water weighs 64 lb.

It is therefore plain that the pressure of water at the depth of a mile must be enormous.   We live at the bottom of an atmospheric ocean, and the air presses on us to the amount of 15 lb. on every square inch of our bodies.   We are unconscious of this, because of the air within us of the same pressure which resists that from outside.   In the sea, at a mile depth the pressure is rather over a ton on the square inch.   It is difficult for a diver to work long at only 30 fathoms in a properly fitted dress, for the pressure outside is 80 lb. on the square inch, whilst he is being supplied with air at a little over 15 lb. inside the dress.   At the greatest depth yet attained by sounding, the pressure must be 6½ tons on the square inch.

How, then, do fish live and move freely in the great depths ? Because their bones are fibrous and hollow, and their tissues are loose and contain water of similar pressure to that outside them.   In the early years of last century it was considered that no life could possibly exist at great depths, as it was presumed that every creature would be flattened out and unable to move.

Another fallacy which has hardly yet died out is that things thrown overboard in deep water never sink to the bottom, but come to rest somewhere in mid-depths, and that if you could descend to those regions you would come across old wrecks and bodies of seamen sewn up in canvas, etc., in suspension, neither rising nor falling.   What really happens

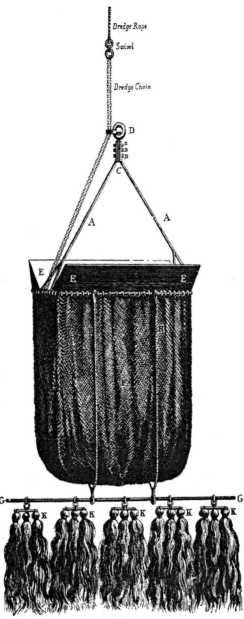

Fig. 3. Dredge.

is that if the article is compressible it is compressed until it becomes much denser and heavier, and all the air in it is ejected. There is then nothing to prevent it sinking, for water is practically non-compressible. The increase of buoyancy at great depths is only about 0·3 per cent., and although the water may be very dense below the article, it is not appreciably less dense above it, and so the weight tells and the sinking continues.

Depth		Pressure		Salinity per 1000		Density
At surface	..	nil	..	36·44	..	1·02525
,, 1000 fathoms	..	1·2 tons	..	34·94	..	1·02770
,, 2000 ,,	..	2·4 ,,	..	34·90	..	1·02800

There is less viscosity in warm sea water than in cold; therefore the sinking body may go slower when it gets down to the cold substratum, but that it gets there is evidenced by the bottom deposits being entirely composed of the remains of the minute life that fills the upper layers of the ocean, and that are fully described in Chapter VIII.

When the *Challenger* sent down a new trawl-beam to 1500 fathoms, it came up so much compressed that the hard knots in the wood stood out an inch or two above the new surface.

When one of the strong brass water-collecting cylinders was sent down accidentally closed, instead of open, to 300 fathoms, it came up again flattened out, the internal air and the cylindrical shape being insufficient to resist the terrific pressure.

One of the American scientific expeditions experimented with hollow glass balls of various thicknesses of glass. These were penetrated and filled, the water forcing its way through the pores of the glass.

Mr. J. Y. Buchanan, F.R.S., late of H.M.S. *Challenger*, has so perfected the deep-sea pressure-gauge that it forms an excellent check on the accuracy of a sounding.

Sir William Thomson's sounding machine, used upon all large vessels, is constructed upon the principle that a record of the pressure will indicate the depth. The known compressibility of air is made use of, the water being admitted into a tube of air closed at one end and compressing it to an amount that can be read off on a scale. Whether the sounding weight touches bottom or not the ship has the negative evidence of a certain depth of water below her.

Deep-sea fish are provided with air inflating bladders. If any such fish in full chase after its prey happens to ascend beyond a certain level its bladder becomes distended owing to

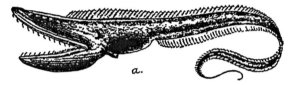

From Brit. Mus. Cat.

FIG. 4A. Deep-sea Fish, *Gastrostomus bairdi*.

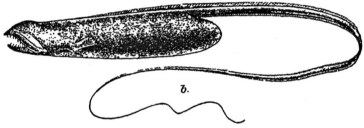

From Brit. Mus. Cat.

FIG. 4B. Deep-sea Fish, *Saccopharynx flagellum*.

the decreased outward pressure. This increases its buoyancy and it is carried in spite of all its efforts still higher in its course. In fact, as Mr. A. P. Crouch points out, these unfortunate animals die a violent death from falling upwards. Their distorted bodies, with the air bladder swollen and projecting from the mouth, are found floating on the surface early in the morning before the scavenger gulls have scoured the seas.

An interesting case, reported by Mr. C. T. Regan, occurred of an angler-fish that lives at about 500 fathoms being found at the surface helpless, having swallowed a fish as large as itself. No doubt the increased displacement, owing to the

B

great distension of its body, forced it to the surface against its will.

The great pressure already mentioned is sufficient to force the water into almost any geological formation. This is probably how sea water finds its way to heated beds, is turned into steam and causes eruptions or earthquakes.

It may be noted that nearly all volcanoes are in the vicinity of the sea. It is almost unthinkable what the pressure must be a short distance within the earth's crust. Granite crumbles under a weight equal to that of a mile thickness of granite. Yet a mile depth is only skin deep compared to the earth's radius. When we are told that a cubic inch of water becomes, when heated to boiling-point, 1645 cubic inches of steam, we can realize why disruption takes place.   A. C.

FIG. 5.   Bringing shark on board (*Challenger*).

CHAPTER II

LIFE IN THE OCEAN

IT is considered that the birthplace of all animal and plant life lay in the sea and then spread to dry land. Some warm-blooded animals, such as whales and porpoises, have again taken to the sea. Life in the deep depends upon the supply of food and on the temperature, and is also governed by the scarcity of oxygen. In an enclosed sea where food debris is abundant from the surrounding land, and where the bottom temperature is comparatively high, life at the bottom is also abundant.

Certain forms of life, which in high latitudes live in cold shallow waters, are found in the low temperatures of the great depths near the equator. They cannot readily change the depth at which they live any more than we can suddenly reside at a height of 10,000 feet, but the adaptation to pressure is not a lengthy process. There is a great deal more general life in shallow water than in deep, owing to a greater supply of food and the presence of light, which encourages the growth of marine plants.

Fig. 6. Manganese nodule, 3000 fathoms, with living Ascidians and Brachiopod attached.

What we call seaweed seldom exists below 30 fathoms, but there are minute plants called unicellular algæ which are microscopic and are particularly abundant as far down as light penetrates. They are of the greatest importance in the

19

economy of the sea. They live parasitically on deep-sea corals, on Globigerina and Radiolaria (*see* Chapter VIII), and, as diatoms, at all depths ; and thus are able to thrive without the aid of sunlight.

In the cruise of the *Michael Sars* in the North Atlantic in 1910 it was found that the pelagic (open ocean) life was always practically identical at corresponding depths.

From the surface down to 75 fathoms there were larvæ and young fish, fish eggs, amphipods, copepods and other crustacea, all colourless ; also Velella, Ianthina and Physalia, blue or transparent, and foraminifera (*see* Chapter VIII).

From 150 to 250 fathoms silvery fish were much in evidence ; fish with telescopic eyes ; the remarkable little fish *Cyclothona signata* ; and several species of red prawns. The silvery fishes are dark on the back and somewhat laterally compressed.

From 500 to 1000 fathoms blacker coloured fish, dark brown medusæ, and different species of red prawns.

At certain stations, such as the rise of the bank on which the Azores Islands stand, there was abundant life even at 1500 fathoms.

The dry land of our globe has gone through many changes of climate, and ubiquitous man has exploited its forests, so that the beasts and birds have in the course of ages died out or evolved new forms, and the present life only dates back to the last geological period. But the ocean, as far as we can judge, has had its fauna less changed, and its great depths retain many ancient forms of life but very slightly altered. Its floor has been merely tickled with the dredge and trawl and yet we can number already 500,000 species, although 400,000 of them are minute and low down in the scale of nature. The larger and more active life declines to be caught in the sluggish trawl, which creeps over the bottom in a cloud of mud-bestirred water. Very remarkable are some of the forms which live in this under-world. The deep-sea fishes (*see* Fig. 4), with their long, narrow, eel-like bodies, large heads and heavy jaws laden with sharp teeth. They are always carnivorous. Their eggs are sometimes found on the surface, so perhaps they come up in the spawning season. Of course the eggs might float up from the bottom, but if they did it hardly seems likely that they would escape destruction on the way.

The *Challenger* made a haul of deep-sea fish in comparatively shallow water in Japan. It was on a line of volcanic

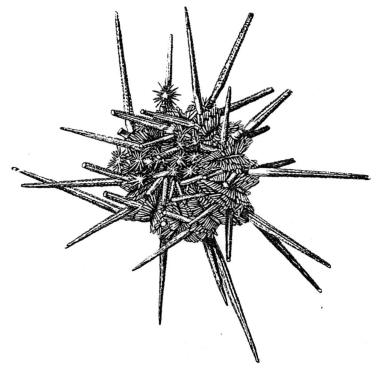

Fig. 7. Sea-egg, with young attached.

energy, so possibly they had been driven up by noxious gases in the water. Deep-water fish feed to some extent on the microscopic life referred to in Chapter VIII. It is impossible to more than touch on a few types of life in that strange under-world. There are spider crabs with bodies only the size of a saucer, but with legs two feet long. Holothurians of all shapes, mostly like soft dirty sausages, with a beautiful crown of tentacles, and wonderful anchor-shaped hooks on their leathery skins. They feed on the bottom mud as our worms feed on our top soils. Sea-eggs (Fig. 7) of all shapes and colours, having a wonderful system of spines working on ball-and-socket joints, and a remarkable parrot's beak and masticating

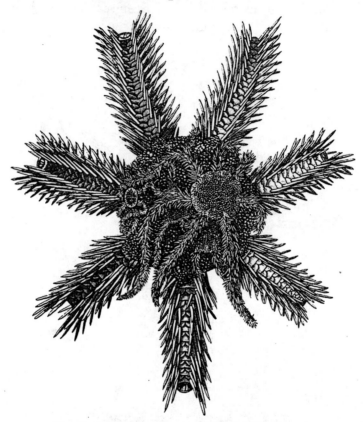

Fig. 8. Ophiurid, with young attached (*Challenger*).

apparatus like Aristotle's lantern. Moving slowly over rock or ground nothing comes amiss to those jaws.

The star-fishes (Fig. 8), closely allied to the last, of all shapes and hues, with their water-vascular feet which can be distended at will and their remarkable power of reproducing a lost limb. The larvæ and young of all these are so strange, that for many years they were considered to belong to different genera of animals.

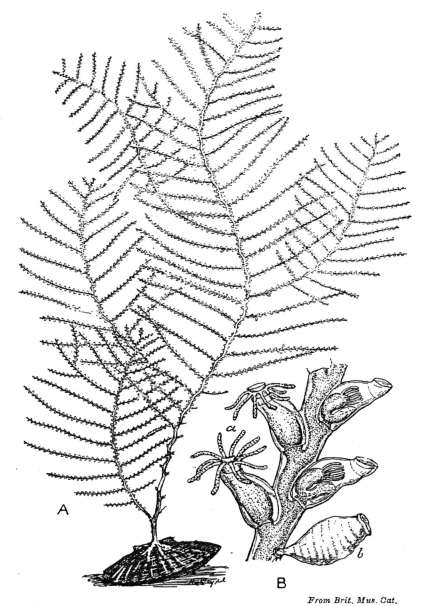

A

B

Fig. 9. Sertularia. A. Slightly enlarged. B. Branchlet, magnified.
a. Polyps. *b*. Reproductive capsule (original).

Then there are those wonderful jellies, the Medusæ, the Siphonophoræ and others, referred to in Chapter VIII, transparent as glass yet with swimming, digestive, and reproducing powers. Sometimes they are colonies of zoophytes, such as Siphonophora, with a common swimming bladder to support them, clusters of feeding zooids, and clusters of generating zooids. Sometimes they are single individuals, the butterfly stage of a colony such as the Sea-fir called Sertularia (Fig. 9). This can often be picked up on the beach near high water mark and will present the appearance of a delicate branching weed with little nicks or jags on the fronds, and sometimes small bladders like fruit on a tree. Instead of the usual oily surface of a weed it is more like horse-hair to the touch. It is known as a Hydrozoon, and the nicks contain zooids that live and work together in a colony. And just as the caterpillar passes through the stages of chrysalis and butterfly, so this pretty miniature tree has gone through the flitting stage of the delicate many-tinted jelly-fish or Hydromedusa. The process is this. The jelly-fish lays an egg which settles on some rock or shell, and soon develops into a little sexless Hydroid tube. This commences to bud, and grow by further budding until the little tree is formed. All the buds connect by channels to the main trunk and branches, and the zooids in the nicks collect their microscopic food by tentacles, and by stinging thread cells with which they lasso and paralyse their prey. Special zooid buds are developed to reproduce the species. The little fruit-like bladders (Fig. 9 b) are the special buds ready to burst and liberate the embryos. They come out as freeswimming oval bodies covered with ciliæ, and at first swim about independently. They then fix themselves by one end to a suitable object, the other end grows and develops a mouth and tentacles. The body elongates, grooves form round it and deepen, and it becomes lobed (Fig. 10). Finally the grooves work right through and a number of saucer-shaped medusæ float off. These are of all shapes and sizes, varying as their parental tree-forms vary, and they eat voraciously as they flap their

FIG. 10. Life History of Jelly-fish (Aurelia). A. Hydra tube. B, C'. Same undergoing transverse division (enlarged). D, D'. Ephyra stage, E, E'. Young Aurelia. F. Fully-grown Aurelia.

phosphorescent way through the water. In the end they lay their eggs, and then, their work done, they die. The egg develops into the Hydro-tube, and history repeats itself.

One of the most remarkable metamorphoses in ocean life is that of the young barnacle which swims about before it settles to the adult fixed stage. The larvæ of the Sea-egg, and of the compound ascidians, go through equally interesting changes.

There are three kinds of life in the sea: the bottom living life ; the pelagic life, from the bottom right up to the surface ; and the partly pelagic, such as the Hydromedusæ.

" Plankton " is the term used for all floating organisms which are passively carried along by currents.

Then there are not only the shell fish that we know so well in shallow waters, but there are many forms that are naked, that is devoid of a distinct shell, like slugs, though often still possessing a rudimentary one.

We are gradually getting to know something of the habits and development of fish, and such knowledge has been of great benefit to our fisheries. It is understood now that the common eel only develops in the open sea, and that all our mature fresh-water eels work their way into the Atlantic and spawn in deep water south of the Azores—at least that is the only place where the transparent glass-like fry of the eel (called Leptocephalus) is found. They come to the surface there and are carried to England, and to Norway, by the currents, and find their way up rivers, and streams, and drain pipes, into quiet reaches and ponds.

The reproduction of young is extraordinarily great, and but for the destruction of eggs and larvæ the ocean would become stiff with fish. The herring, a most useful article of food to man, produces some 30,000 eggs per annum, and the cod several million.

In Samoa, Fiji, Florida, and Japan there is a thin worm that lives in coral and other rock below low tide level. It is called Eunice or Palolo. On certain days of the year, shortly before sunrise, there is a sudden appearance on the surface

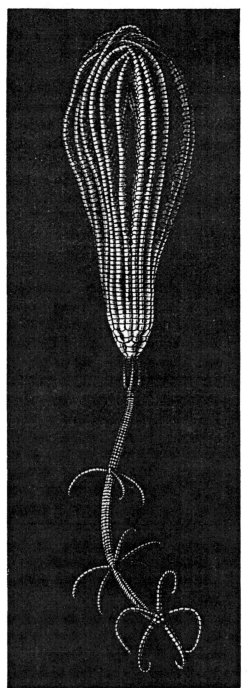

Fig. 11. A Crinoid (*Challenger*).

of countless swarms of young expelled into the water, and these are seen wriggling violently and are collected as food by man.

We quote these instances of life in the ocean not so much to give an exact description of them, but to remind the reader how different, owing to difference of conditions, life beneath the waters must be from that on dry land. In the following chapters many other forms will be referred to.

In Chapter VIII will be found some account of the surface life that may be seen by a careful observer from the deck of a becalmed vessel, and many a weary hour may under those circumstances be enlivened by lowering a boat and carefully dipping a bucket or glass jar under some of the delicate forms.

When deep-sea dredging was first satisfactorily carried out, a very interesting discovery was that of living forms, such as Crinoids, that had only been previously known in their fossil state. Several of the most beautiful forms date back to the Carboniferous period, and their remains can be plentifully found in the Peak country in Derbyshire. The Natural History Museum at South Kensington has a very fine collection of Crinoids (Figs. 11 and 12), which will well repay a visit.

The ocean is so immense, and its contents so well hidden from our sight, that we can form but a poor opinion as to the frequency or rarity of a species. The Prince of Monaco used a trap at 700 fathoms in which he caught in one haul no less than 1200 Symenchelys. The *Challenger* only caught one or two of these fish. Cuttle-fish are seldom seen in great numbers, yet bushels of their horny beaks are found in the stomachs of whales. A sperm whale has been known to throw up, when harpooned, one of the arms of a cuttle-fish which, though not complete, was 29 feet in length.

The herbivorous deep-sea animals (all very small) live on the minute algæ already referred to, and they in turn are food for the carnivorous animals that form the majority.

At a certain depth where wave action is not felt and tidal

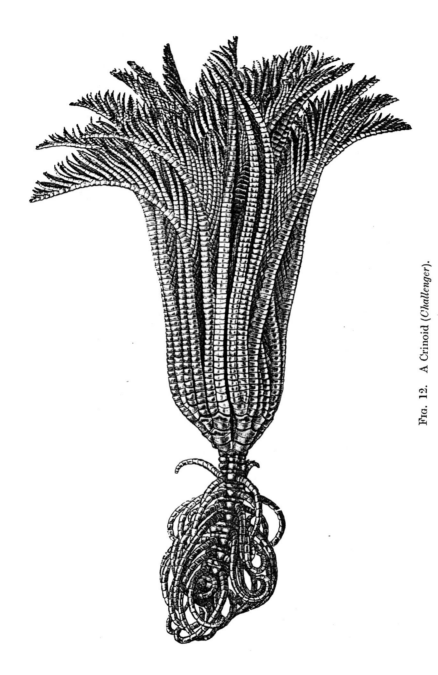

Fig. 12. A Crinoid (*Challenger*).

action makes no movement, mud commences to settle on the bottom. It is this depth that forms the finest feeding-ground for all bottom-living animals, such as holothurians, sea-eggs, and star-fish; but the coral zooid will not grow in this mud, as it is easily killed by silt. A. C.

Fig. 13. Commercial Sponges (*Euspongia officinalis mollissima*).

CHAPTER III

MAMMALS

Polar Bears. Occasionally, near the edge of the northern ice-pack, a passing ship may sight a polar bear in sorry plight adrift on an ice floe in the Atlantic.

The polar bear—the one land animal ever met with at sea

Photo R. C. Mossman, F.R.S.E.

Fig. 14. Polar Bear getting up on an ice floe.

—is a fierce, active creature, a powerful swimmer and climber, equally at home in the water and on the ice.

Hair on the padded soles of its feet gives the animal its surprising ease and grip in climbing the most slippery ice

31

floes and bergs, and its sure-footed swiftness in clambering among them. It lives chiefly on seals, porpoises, and fish,

From Brit. Mus. Cat.

Fig. 15.   Northern Fur Seal, male and female.

From Brit. Mus. Cat.

Fig. 16.   The Common Seal.

and takes kindly also to a vegetable diet when that comes in its way.

Seals and Sea Lions. Curiously enough, while fishes of all sorts and ocean animal life in general seem lacking in intelligence, seals—the one exception to the rule—are extraordinarily alert and teachable. They are easily tamed, and make interesting pets in captivity. They have finely formed heads and large brilliant eyes, well adapted evidently to seeing under water. Their sense of smell is acute, also their hearing, although their organs of hearing are hidden beneath the skin.

Musical sounds are said to attract and fascinate them.

Their so-called feet are more accurately swimming paddles, stretched out behind the body, parallel with the tail. Admirably effective in the water, their hind limbs are useless on land, where the fore limbs or flippers come into play. Handicapped for land travel as they are physically, seals can climb slippery rocks with ease, and they manage to get over ground very rapidly, with a curious wriggling movement. A herd of seals in the water or on rocks is an interesting sight.

In the intervals of swimming they are fond

Photo H. G. Herring

FIG. 17. Sea Lion.

of clambering on to rocks, where they lie sunning themselves with evident enjoyment. They swim with extraordinary rapidity and ease in any position, and, like the cetacea, they dive and swim without disturbing the water or creating waves, or any apparent resistance. They inhabit all the oceans, but are least numerous in the tropics. The northern sea-bears, from which the best fur is obtained, are practically confined to the Behring Sea districts, where they are now protected by severe international laws restricting seal hunting, which was formerly pursued at all seasons with so much cruel and indiscriminate

c

slaughter that the rapid extinction of the creatures was threatened. Fur seals are found also in the southern hemisphere at Kerguelen Land; on the Australian coasts, the Cape of Good Hope, and the South Shetland Islands. Some Northern sea lions frequent rocks at the entrance to San Francisco harbour, and are an object of interest to passing ships.

Seals breed on land at certain favourite haunts, where they assemble for the purpose. The sight is said to be amazing.

Photo R. C. Mossman, F.R.S.E.
FIG. 18.   Weddell Seal and Young.

The males arrive first and await the coming of the females, which event is the signal for fierce fighting for their possession. The old males only try their luck; the young ones recognize probably the futility of pitting their strength against that of their elders, anyway they do not attempt to dispute the right of might to bear away the prizes. The old males fight for as many mates as they can get—the stronger ones prevailing for, perhaps, some forty females, the weaker securing a fewer number. The battle wages fiercely until all the females are appropriated.

The male guards his mates jealously and fights furiously to defend them and their young. Both parents appear passionately attached to the pups. It is a curious fact that the young seals do not take kindly to the water; their evident reluctance to a cold bath has to be overcome by much coaxing on the part of their elders.

Seals live on animal food exclusively—fish, molluscs, and crustaceans. They are most voracious, and very destructive to food fishes. When displeased, hungry or hurt, seals utter a peculiar sound, half bark and half heart-broken moan, a very disquieting and disturbing noise when heard during the night at sea.

The Whale Family. The *whale* family and its kindred, *grampuses*, *dolphins* and *porpoises*, are the most striking objects in ocean life. Whales are often of gigantic size (a 60 foot whale may weigh 100 tons), are true warm-blooded animals, capable of living on the sea surface and of "sounding," as it is called, to unknown depths.* At times they leap or throw themselves completely into the air.

The skeleton of the whale is loosely jointed; its lungs are large and long, and are able to take in and to hold large supplies of air. Beneath the skin the body is protected by a very thick layer of fat called "blubber." This fat is a heat retainer, and also a buffer between the animal and the greatly increased pressure to which it is subjected when in the depths For the size of the whale the eyes are peculiarly small. The ears, although covered with skin, are extraordinarily sensible to sound. The nostrils are slits in a prominence on the top of the head. In "sounding" they are closed by the external pressure of water. When the whale comes again to the surface, the nostrils expel with much force the exhausted air from the lungs. This *blowing* process throws up the surrounding sea in a jet-like spray. Unlike the tail of a fish, which is in a line with the body, the whale family sport powerful tails " across " or ' ' athwart ship ! "

Usually whales are met with in groups known as "schools." The most commonly seen are the *Greenland* whale, the *Biscayan* whale (Fig. 19), the *Boreal blue* whale, the *Rorqual* or *fin*

* On this point the Prince of Monaco has made interesting observations.

whale (Fig. 20), the *Humpbacked* whale, the *Cachalot* (Fig. 22), and *Bottle-nosed* whales.   The two last named have no " whale-bone " and are squid-eating animals.   The *Greenland* and the *Biscayan* whales feed on the small Plankton * life of the sea

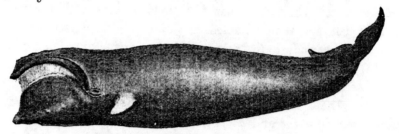

FIG. 19.   The North Atlantic Black Right-Whale (*Balæna glacialis*).

FIG. 20.   The Blue Rorqual (*Balænoptera sibbaldi*).

FIG. 21.   The Humpback Whale (*Megaptera boöps*).
(Fig. 19 about $\frac{1}{127}$, Fig. 20 $\frac{1}{195}$, Fig. 21 $\frac{1}{195}$ natural size.)
By kind permission of the Trustees of the British Museum

surface only.   The *Boreal blue* whale and the *Rorqual* or *fin* whale feed on Plankton and on pelagic fishes.   To trap the minute Plankton life on which these high beasts feed, they have in their mouths, depending from the palate, rows of the horny substance called whalebone.   Through the water to feed

* *See* Glossary.

rushes the whale, open mouthed, taking into his jaws or entangling in the whalebone quantities of Plankton life. To squeeze out the water, the mouth is closed and the great tongue pressed against the whalebone. Vast fields of whale food occur at sea; one met with in the Indian Ocean was perhaps sixty miles long and probably not much less in width. (*See* Chapter VIII.)

The squid-eating whales, *Cachalots* and *Bottle-nosed* whales, are provided with strong teeth in the lower jaw. They seize, tear, and chew up the largest squids, though these often fight gallantly for life and leave the marks of their suckers all over their foe.

There is fascination in the sight of a school of whales swimming close to a ship, gliding, as it were, in and out of the sea with an easy stateliness of movement, scarcely rippling the surface, probably because of the oily substance which coats them and the non-resistance of their body formation to the water. Occasionally the whales " breach," or jump completely clear of the sea, coming down into it again with a resounding thud audible far away. The *Humpbacked* whale has long pectoral fins (20 feet or more), black on one side, white on the other. It has a habit of lying on one side waving its upper fin in the air; this fin shows black at one moment and white the next. In sounding, the animal goes down perpendicularly, the tail standing upright in the water as it disappears.

The Humpbacked whale is found in the largest numbers off the coasts of Brazil.

Whales are met with in all parts of the ocean; apparently they shift continually from place to place, but they are most numerous in the polar seas, where their special food (*Clio borealis*) abounds. Also a small shrimp (Amphipoda), which seems to be a very delicate morsel to the whale, is common in those regions.

The *Sperm* whale frequents all the oceans and all temperate latitudes. In appearance it is very remarkable, owing to

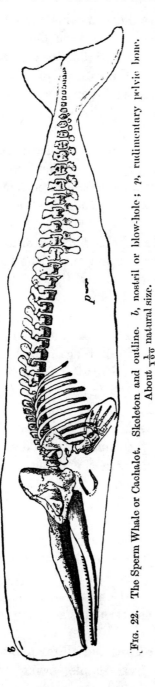

FIG. 22. The Sperm Whale or Cachalot. Skeleton and outline. *b*, nostril or blow-hole; *p*, rudimentary pelvic bone. About $\frac{1}{100}$ natural size.

By kind permission of the Trustees of the British Museum

its huge head (about one-third the animal's length), in which is secreted the valuable spermaceti oil for which this whale is hunted. Ambergris, a substance much used in scent making, is a curious morbid secretion sometimes found in the intestine of the Sperm whale.

On what would seem to be trustworthy evidence, one hears sometimes of combined attacks made on whales by the Threshers (a species of dog-fish) and the Narwhals, or the sword-fish. We have never seen anything of the sort, nor does Bennett, in his very interesting "Whaling Voyage," allude to any such conflict. It seems strange that so curious a fact should have evaded the notice of so acute an observer. It may be, however, that these fights do occur. Swallows and other small birds will not hesitate, one knows, to harry a hawk. It is affirmed that the thresher opens the attack by leaping into the air and alighting on the whale, the latter being kept from "sounding" by the sword-fish on guard beneath its body. The thresher could not possibly—owing to its mouth formation—bite the whale, but in time the tongue of the exhausted victim lolls out, when it is immediately seized by the watching

foe. One wonders how the narwhal or the sword-fish, which
attacks the whale from below, withdraws the " sword " when
the whale is pierced ! To one who has watched the Humpbacked whale gambol, turn, toss, and wave gigantic fins in the
air in sheer exuberance of life, it is not surprising that sailors
should mistake these agitated sword-like fins, now white, now
black, for tormenting foes.

Undoubtedly schools of grampuses (Fig. 25) do at times attack

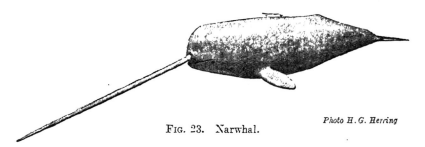

FIG. 23. Narwhal.   *Photo H. G. Herring*

whales, especially when they find one detached, or with a
calf.

There is a whale called a *narwhal* peculiar to the Arctic
seas. It grows sometimes to a length of fifteen feet, and its tusk
to seven feet. This tusk is in reality a tooth, and therefore
of a different nature from the beak of the sword-fish (p. 73).

Whale catching is different now from what it was in earlier
days. Then boats got as near to the sleeping or resting
animal as was safe, harpoons attached to a line were darted
into it, and there followed a scene such as has been well described
—from a scientific point of view—in Bennett's " Wanderings
of a Naturalist " :

The appearance of a spouting or "breaching" whale is
announced by the cry " There she blows ! " or " There she
breaches ! " (the feminine being applied as the epicene gender
of whales), and these exclamations are repeated as often as
the phenomena are exhibited, unless " There again ! " should
be substituted, for the sake of variety or brevity.

As soon as it is ascertained that the whales noticed are the kind required, and placed favourably for attack, the order is given to commence the pursuit ; when less than two minutes suffices to place the boats simultaneously in the water, manned with their respective crews, and pulling energetically, if the whales are to windward. or sailing as well as pulling if the school should be to leeward ; the ship, in the meantime, attending them at a convenient distance, to direct their proceedings by observations made from the masthead, and communicated by an established code of signals.

When a boat has approached a whale within a reasonable distance. the harpooner quits his oar and stands in the bow, with the harpoon in his hand, until the exertions of the rest of the crew have advanced the boat sufficiently close, and in a favourable position to strike.* The first harpoon is then darted and pierces the body of the whale—the second almost instantaneously follows with equal success, and the effects become visible at a great distance, as the wounded monster plunges convulsively, casting its flukes high in the air, and raising clouds of foam and lofty columns of water which obscure and threaten to overwhelm the attacking party. After this first display of surprise and agony, the whale sets off with great swiftness along the surface of the water, drawing after it the attached boat ; the line being secured around the logger-head, her oars apeak and bristling from either side, and her bow raised high above the level of the sea and enveloped in spray ; whilst the water, displaced by the velocity of her motion, rises on each side of the depressed stern, considerably above the level of the gunwale, threatening an inundation which she appears only to evade by her speed.

About this time the officer in command resigns the steer-oar to the harpooner, and takes his station in the bow of the boat, where, armed with the lance, he avails himself of every opportunity to haul up close to the whale and dart his weapon into its body.

Finding flight in the horizontal direction insufficient for escape, the whale endeavours to elude his pursuers by "sounding," or descending perpendicularly to a great depth ; but this attempt is equally ineffectual with the first, and after a short interval he reappears on the surface, the boat again approaches, and the attack with the lance is renewed, until

---

* The whale is approached from the tail end.

exhausted by loss of blood, and his strenuous endeavours to escape, the animal becomes perceptibly more feeble in his movements, the sea for some distance around is crimsoned with his blood, and the spout (also mingled with blood) as it rises at each aspiration, is scattered conspicuously in the air, like shreds of scarlet cloth. After the slow pace of the whale and his general air of languor, as well as the jets of dark blood cast from his spiracle scarce higher than the crests of the waves, would lead to the idea that his efforts are at an end, he again draws the attached boat rapidly over the water and the contest appears to be renewed ; but this is merely the last struggle of the dying Cachalot, or, as it is termed, " the flurry," and hurrying about, beating the waves with its tail, the creature takes a circuitous rather than a direct course —then turns on his side—his lower jaw falls—and the " monarch of the flood " floats a lifeless mass, over which the waves beat with a low and confused surf. . . ."

Thrilling stories of whale fishing are told in "Moby Dick " and in the " Cruise of the Cachalot."

Whaling in these times was a perilous and exciting adventure requiring skill and pluck to face and to carry through.

Now small steam vessels fitted with harpoon guns in the bows and with apparatus for inflating the slaughtered whale that it may not sink and get lost, quickly and quietly steam up to the resting whale. A harpoon is discharged at close range and a bomb finishes the animal. The carcase is then towed to a cutting-up wharf.

One cannot but regret that the persistent fishing, carried on in this " scientific " way, will gradually exterminate whales * of any commercial value. Were these animals more intelligent they would possibly learn to evade destruction, but a whale seldom shows a glimmer of sense. Attacks on its young alone seem to awaken this faculty.

* Whale fishing appears to be quite abandoned now by the British. The Norwegians keep it up. One hundred and eighty-three whales were captured in 1906. Twelve thousand six hundred and thirty-five whales were captured in 1911 in Southern waters alone. This wholesale destruction of whales, unless checked, may result in unforeseen but serious disturbance of the balance of life in the sea.

Frank Bullen tells the story that one day, by accident, a harpoon killed a calf, with the result that the infuriated mother sank fifty whaling boats of a fleet of fifty-two, killed seven men and injured seventeen.

Many whales lose their lives through stranding. For instance, seventeen sperm whales went ashore off the Elbe in December 1723; thirty-two sperm whales at Audierne, France, during a storm in 1784, and thirty-seven sperm whales at Perkins Island, Tasmania, in 1911. Of these last, thirty-six were males. One hundred caaing whales were driven ashore at Thurso in 1899. Thereabouts it is quite usual to capture whales by driving them inshore from the sea. Whales have been found entangled in telegraph cables. Sometimes a ship runs into one asleep on the surface.

The old whalers told some awe-inspiring tales of their occasional encounter with unusually large and ferocious whales. It is probable that such monsters did at times hold the sea for long against all attempts at capture. Early in the last century, such a brute, a cachalot, became well known as "New Zealand Tom"; he was distinguished by a white hump, and was a terror to whalers off the New Zealand coasts. Some time later another huge whale infested the same waters.

In fiction no story is more thrilling than that of "Moby Dick, or The White Whale," by Herman Melville.

It is astonishing that no sportsman has taken to the hunting of the bigger and more ferocious whales on old-fashioned lines. The most intrepid would get quite as much if not more excitement and peril as he could wish, and no big game hunt could excel such a whale chase in sheer fascination of pursuit.

A highly tragical instance of the power and ferocity occasionally displayed by the sperm whale is recorded in the fate of the American South Seaman *Essex*, Captain G.

Pollard. This vessel, when cruising in the Pacific Ocean in the year 1820, was wrecked by a whale under the following extraordinary circumstances. The boats had been lowered in pursuit of a school of whales, and the ship was attending them to windward. The master and second mate were engaged with whales they had harpooned, in the midst of the school, and the chief mate had returned on board to equip a spare boat in lieu of his own, which had been broken and rendered unserviceable. While the crew were thus occupied, the lookout at the masthead reported that a large whale was coming rapidly down upon the ship, and the mate hastened his task in the hope that he might be ready in time to attack it.

The Cachalot, which was of the largest size, consequently a male, and probably the guardian of the school, in the meanwhile approached the ship so closely that, although the helm was put up to avoid the contact, he struck her a severe blow, which broke off a portion of her keel. The enraged animal was then observed to retire to some distance, and again rush upon the ship with extreme velocity. His enormous head struck the starboard bow, beating in a corresponding portion of the planks, and the people on board had barely time to take to their boat before the ship filled with water and fell over on her side. She did not sink, however, for some hours ; and the crew in the boats continued near the wreck until they had obtained a small supply of provisions, when they shaped a course for land. . . .

One of the most extraordinary encounters with a whale is that related by Captain Dias of the U.S. whaleship *Pocahontas* on December 12, 1850, in the S. Atlantic.

A school of sperm whales was sighted and boats put off to capture. A whale was struck, but turned on the boat and wrecked it. The crew escaped by swimming to the other boat. The whale remained by the wrecked boat. The crew went back on board their ship, which they sailed down on the whale with the intention of lancing or harpooning it from the deck. But the whale, apparently guessing what was coming, charged the ship on the starboard bow, breaking a couple of timbers and causing such a leak that the vessel had to abandon the fight and make at once for the Port of Rio de Janeiro.

FIG. 24. A Grampus.

By kind permission of the Trustees of the British Museum

On September 17, 1852, a French vessel, the *Pauline*, 400 tons, was struck by a whale and sunk in fifteen minutes.   The crew

FIG. 25.   A School of Grampus.

By kind permission of Professor Takayanagi, Chief of the Nautical College, Tokyo

barely had time to escape. The ship, laden with sugar, was on her way from Porto Rico to Havre.

Only as recently as May 6, 1914, in the North Atlantic, the Elder Dempster liner *Sangara* was stopped for three quarters of an hour by a whale which had got its head jammed between the propeller and stern-post, and it took some time to get it clear.

Naturalists are eager for more knowledge of the habits of whales. Squids, which are the principal food of the sperm whale or Cachalot, evidently are much more numerous than

Photo by E. C. Youens

Fig. 26.   Dolphin.

we are aware of, living probably in the intermediate depths of the sea.

The *Grampus*, Killer or Orca (Fig. 24), is a ferocious monster, often thirty feet long and having an enormous dorsal fin. It wanders about in small schools, attacking anything from a whale to its own kind.   In search of seals the grampus will stand almost upright in the water to overlook an ice floe.   Should a quarry be discovered, the entire school will join forces to capsize the floe and precipitate the seal into the water, when they immediately tear it to pieces.*

Dolphins congregate in large schools.   They may be met near the coasts or far out at sea.   A white species of dolphin is seen in the river mouths and harbours on the coasts of China.

* In the annals of the Antarctic Expedition of Captain Scott, the late Lieut. H. R. Bowers, R.I.M., gives a thrilling account of the hunting of seals among ice floes by schools of grampuses.

Porpoises keep permanently near the coasts.

As shown in the illustrations, the dolphin is slimmer of body and has a longer snout than the porpoise ; also, its custom is to leap clean out of the water, while the porpoises' apparently

Photo by Capt. Wilson-Barker
FIG. 27.   A Dolphin jumping.

are content with rolling over in the sea.   The play of dolphins round a ship, particularly beneath the bows, is a very enter-

FIG. 28.   Porpoise.
By kind permission of the Trustees of the British Museum

taining sight.   Some excellent sport may be had in a sailing-ship by trying to harpoon them from the dolphin strike (*see* p. 72).

In the high southern latitudes a *piebald dolphin* (*Delphinapterus Peronei*) is met with, and probably the remarkable "Pelorus Jack" which haunts Cook Strait, New Zealand, belongs to this variety.*

* It is reported to have disappeared, probably destroyed by a whaler.

CHAPTER IV

BIRDS AND REPTILES

Of living creatures, birds are the most frequently met with at sea.

The *Gull* family, which includes many varieties, is widely

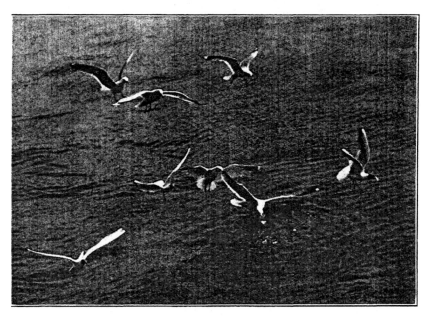

Photo by Charles Kirk

Fig. 29. Common and Black-headed Gulls.

distributed and is familiar to all coast visitors. These birds may be termed coast dwellers, as they constantly frequent the shore, taking occasional long flights to sea; and sometimes, more especially in hard weather, penetrating far inland. Their appearance is hailed by ships as an early sign of land. In the old days, sailing-ship seamen nicknamed the gulls "Boarding-house runners," knowing that after them would come the "touts" on the look-out for "Jack from sea," to bear him and his purse off to one of their haunts. Many oceanic islands, as well as others close to land, are frequented by

D. W.-B.

Fig. 30. Black-backed Gull.

gulls in thousands for breeding purposes. In common with other sea birds, the gulls are long in attaining their permanent plumage; this fact and that there are many varieties of gulls render their identification difficult. The best known sorts are the *Common Gull*, the *Black-headed Gull*, the *Black-backed Gull*, the *Kitti-wake*, the *Herring Gull*, and the *Skua Gull*. This last named may be classed practically among the oceanic birds. It is fierce and predaceous, not hesitating to attack the giant albatross in dispute of food. It is very destructive to the eggs and young of other birds. The skua gull is easily recognized by its sharply hooked beak and dark brown plumage with whitish bars on the wing.

Photo, R. C. Mossman, F.R.S.E.

FIG. 31. Skua Gulls.

The distinguishing feature of different varieties of gull is often indicated in the name of the bird.

FIG. 32. Arctic Tern on Nest. *C. Kirk*

The *Tern* or Sea Swallow is a small gull of slender build, rather long pointed wings, and a sharp straight back. In colour it is a pearly grey or white. The *Noddy*, a dark species

D

FIG. 33.   Cormorant.

By kind permission o   C. Griffin and Co.

of gull, is found in the tropics and southern seas. These birds sometimes settle on sailing-ships and get caught. They have been known to make their own way into the cabins below.

Cormorants and *Shags* have long powerful bodies, snake-like necks, and long hooked beaks. They are a glossy blue-black in colour. The Shags are slightly crested. Common to all coasts, these birds are voracious feeders, and when gorged with food may be seen perched on rocks with partially ex-

Fig. 34. Gannets or Solan Geese.   *Photo by Charles Kirk*

tended wings. They catch fish with ease and rapidity. In China and Japan they are often trained to " hawk " fish from the decks of junks. The food of the young birds is partly predigested in the stomach of the mother. The little ones put their heads into the parent bird's mouth to feed.

Quite recently Professor H. O. Forbes has been making some investigations in the islands off the coast of Peru in which the cormorants breed in millions. It appears that these islands are a great source of revenue to the government, from the amount of guano found there. Suddenly all the grown birds departed, leaving thousands of young—in all stages of growth —to die a miserable death. Where they went to or why they left so suddenly, are mysteries. It seems that they returned again some months later. Among other observations, Professor Forbes estimated that in one congregation of cormorants fishing off the coast there were over ten million birds ; as each bird

Photo by the late Lieut. H. R. Bowers, R.I.M.

Fig. 35. Frigate Birds.

eats about ten pounds of fish per day, one realizes somewhat the quantities of fish they consume.

Gannets (Fig. 34) are strong handsome birds with sharp beaks. They are often met with far out at sea, and sometimes are caught asleep on the yards of a ship. In fishing this bird flies high above the water, into which it drops like a stone on its prey, immediately regaining its high point of observation. It is a voracious bird, and when caught often disgorges quantities of whole fishes.

Gannets breed in numbers on the Bass Rock and in Maine Island of North-East Australia. The adult bird is white with a yellow head. It is about 3 feet long, with a wing spread of 6 feet, and may weigh seven pounds. This bird is well furnished with air cells beneath the skin. These are entirely under its control and are the main factor in its powerful flight.

The *Booby* is of the gannet family, and like that bird in characteristics and habits, but is different in colouring, being white breasted, with dark brown back and practically black head and throat. Its young are brown all over.

The *Frigate Bird* has large powerful wings and a long forked tail. Its beak is hooked like an eagle's. The plumage is

Fig. 36. Bo'sun Bird.

brown, with white throat and a red pouch. The Frigate bird is a true oceanic bird, though frequently met with near land owing to its habit of flying with gulls to rob them of their food. It does this by snatching fish from the gull's beak as that bird rises from the sea with its prey. The frigate bird breeds on lonely rocks and among coral islands.

The *Bo'sun, Marlinspike* or *Tropic Bird* is smaller than the common gull and more like a sea swallow in form. Two long reddish feathers in the tail suggest somewhat a marlinspike. Like the frigate bird it flies high, and like the gannet it drops from a height on its prey. These birds are met with sometimes in mid-ocean. They look graceful and peaceful creatures as they soar above a ship. Their breeding-places are oceanic islands.

The *Sheath-bill* or " Paddy " bird is met with off the

Falkland Islands, and between the Cape and Australia. It is a beautiful white bird not unlike a gull.

The *Little Auk* or *Rotch*, *Guillemots*, and *Puffins* are swim-

FIG. 37. Guillemot.

FIG. 38. Puffin.

ming and diving birds which catch their food easily under water. They frequent the coasts in large numbers.

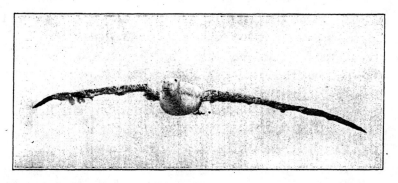

D.W.-B.

FIG. 39. Wandering Albatross.

The *Rotch* is a neat little bird about 8 inches long, glossy black above, white beneath.

The *Guillemot* is about 18 inches long and is similar in

colouring, with a larger, sharper beak, has a wing spread of $2\frac{1}{4}$ feet and weighing $1\frac{1}{2}$ lb. It lays a handsome egg, big for the size of the bird, and varying much in colour though not in shape or size.

Photo by Lieut. *H. R. Bowers, R.I.M.*

Fig. 40. Wandering Albatross.

Puffins with their parrot-like beaks are plump quaint little birds—a puffin rookery is well worth a visit.

The *true Oceanic birds* are :

The Petrels,	*Fulmars,*
Albatrosses,	*Shearwaters,*
Giant Petrels,	*Cape Pigeons,*
Molly Mawks,	*Whale Birds,*

and the Little Stormy Petrels.

Of these the albatross is the most interesting and is of many sorts. They are chiefly birds of the southern oceans, though two species are met with in the North Pacific. All have long narrow wings, short tails, powerful yellow beaks and thick plumage. The largest is the *Wandering Albatross* with a wing-spread of from 6 feet 7 inches to 10 feet 6 inches.

The smaller varieties are the *Molly Mawks* and *Sooty Albatrosses* with a wing-spread of from 6 feet 6 inches to 7 feet.   A large

D.W.-B

FIG. 41.   Molly Mawk.

Photo by Lieut. H. R. Bowers, R.I.M.

FIG. 42.   Sooty Albatross.

albatross may weigh 24 lb., a small one from 6 to 8 lb.   As with other sea birds, the predominant colouring is black and white.   The plumage varies more in the larger than in

the smaller kinds. The sooty albatross is always of a dark
sooty brown hue.

These birds are most numerous between 38° and 45° south

D.W.-B.

Fig. 43.   Giant Petrel.

latitude. They frequently accompany ships for long distances,
maintaining their position apparently without effort or much
perceptible movement of wing.   It has been suggested that

Fig. 44.   Shearwater.

the birds sleep in their flight, but it seems more likely that
they can go for long periods without rest. Except in the
breeding season, the albatrosses live at sea.

When angry, and always when captured on board ship,
these birds eject from their beaks a peculiar foul-smelling oil.

The *Giant Petrel*, though larger and heavier in build, closely resembles the sooty albatross. The *Fulmar Petrel* is akin to the giant petrel, but it inhabits the Northern hemisphere. It is,

FIG. 45.   Cape Pigeon.

however, smaller in size and grey and white in colouring. A peculiarly thick nostril is characteristic of all the petrel tribe.

The *Shearwaters*, a group of smaller petrels, are of world-wide distribution. Sailors call them " Mutton " birds. They

FIG. 46.   Whale Bird.

are a brownish grey, and are about the size of a duck, and are named from their habit of flying close to the surface. They have what seems to be a quick untiring flight, but they do not follow ships.

The *Cape Pigeons* are the most conspicuous and the most common birds of the high southern latitudes. They accompany ships in hundreds, and in calm weather as they alight on the surface have been caught by hand from the rail of a rolling vessel. Usually, however, these birds are trapped in a thread weighted with shot and blown out astern. The writer once caught in this way, and released, 170 in twelve hours. They are pretty mottled black-and-white birds.

Fig. 47. Stormy Petrel at home.

Whale Birds or *Prions* are smaller than Cape pigeons and are as numerous. They are hard to capture, have a rapid zigzag flight and go about in flocks. Their plumage is bluish grey and their beaks are broad and boat shaped.

Mother Carey's Chickens or the *Stormy Petrels* are met with everywhere at sea. They are small black birds with white bars over their tails. They flutter, rather than fly, over the surface with hanging legs which often seem to tread or run up a wave. In movement they are more suggestive of butterflies than of birds.

FIG. 48.   Great Northern Diver.   *D. W.-B.*

Photo R. C. Mossman, F.R.S.E.

FIG. 49.   Adélie Penguins and Young.

All the *Petrel* group swim well but do not dive. They nest in burrows in the ground on oceanic islands.

The *Great Northern Diver* is a handsome bird as large as a

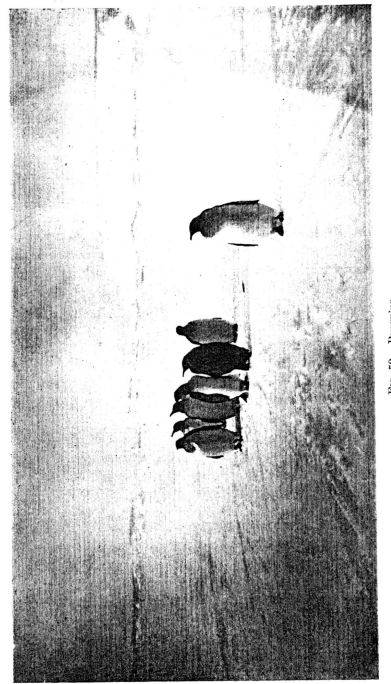

FIG. 50. Penguins.

By kind permission of Société d'Océanographie de Golf de Gasgogne

goose, with glossy black plumage, spotted white. It is met with sometimes far out at sea.

The *Penguins* are non-flying birds which live at sea almost as continuously as do the albatrosses. Off the Falkland Islands and in other localities in the southern ocean they may be seen in thousands, often making a curious cry like a little bark. A flock disturbed by a ship will hurry off, jumping in and out of the water exactly like a school of small dolphins. They use their little winglets and their feet in swimming. On land they walk upright with a leisurely waddling gait. But if flurried or hurried, they drop on their breasts and then with the help of their winglets scurry along at a good pace.

The penguins vary much in size, from the little *Rock Hopper* to the *Emperor Penguin*, which stands 3½ feet high and weighs up to 80 lb. Some species are gaily decorated with tufts and crests of coloured feathers. All have the pure white breasts and black cloak-like plumage which is so ludicrously suggestive of the wrapped-up figures of little old men. The late Captain Scott's recent Antarctic Expedition did much to increase our knowledge of these interesting birds. They are found in the southern hemisphere only. Their breeding-places are on the rocky coasts of islands.

Many strange bird visitants make their appearance from time to time on ships at sea, especially on sailing-vessels. We have known a bittern come on board in mid-Atlantic and live there for some days. In the Mediterranean a flock of quail may pass over a ship or may alight on it. Migrating birds sometimes flock down on board, as has happened in the English channel in foggy weather, when many perish from cold. Not infrequently a hawk or an owl will settle down on a ship, having lost itself in chasing a small bird out to sea.

Sailors have a curious habit of putting odd names to things they see, particularly to birds. For instance, the Albatross has been called the "Cape Sheep," the Sooty Albatross the "Stink Pot," the Giant Petrel the "Cape Hen," the Prions the "Whale Birds," the Cape Petrel the "Cape Pigeon," the smaller Albatross "Molly Hawk" or "Molly Mawk," the Stormy Petrels "Mother Carey's Chickens," and so on. Sailors are, in fact, seldom at a loss for a name for any object a passenger may be curious about.

The following is typical of many dialogues on the decks of vessels at sea :

Æsthetic Passenger (to Old Salt) : "Can you tell me, my good man, the name of that fine bird hovering about ? "

Old Salt : " That's a halba-tross, sir."

Æ. P. : " Dear me ! Quite a *rara avis*, is it not ? "

Old Salt : " Dunno, sir, I've always heard it called a halba-tross."

Æ. P. : " Yes, yes, my good fellow, but I call that a *rara avis*, just as I call you a *genus homo*."

Old Salt (indignantly) : " Oh, do you ? Then I calls that a halbatross, just the same as I calls you an old humbug."

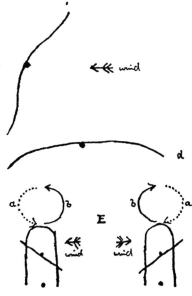

Fig. 51. *c.* Albatross "in a wind." *d.* Albatross flying with or head to a wind. E. Albatross circling round stern of sailing ship : (*a*) close to sea ; (*b*) high in air. They sweep round as indicated in great circular planes without flapping the wings, and in direction of arrow heads.

Flight. At sea there are special opportunities for observations of the wonderful powers of flight of the large oceanic birds. Possibly we may some day discern the secret of their beautiful poise and of the easily maintained floating attitude in which they forge ahead quickly against a dead head wind with but little apparent movement of the wings.* The true oceanic birds, albatrosses, have two distinct methods of positions

* See *Nature* and the *Shipping World*, August 13, 1913, in which papers this matter of sea bird flight has been dealt with in greater detail by the writer.

in flying—" on the wind " and " head to " or " going away "
from the direction of the wind.

With less success both positions are adopted by gulls in flight.

D. W. B.

FIG. 52.   Gulls in flight head to wind.

FIG. 54.   Albatrosses (3 upper
birds) and Frigate Bird (lowest
bird).   Both soar and fly through
the air without flapping or movement of wings.

FIG. 53.   Gulls soaring
and flapping.

It is certain that the secret of birds' flight and the power they
have of sailing as it were in the air, with no apparent effort,
are closely connected with the adoption of these positions.

Some theorists maintain that the birds avail themselves

largely of ascending air currents, etc., but none can explain
the main facts of flight. The great oceanic birds have a
peculiarly thick coating of feathers, containing large reserves
of warm air ; and the bones of these birds though very strong
are light. A large albatross with a wing area of five square
feet may weigh about twenty pounds. It is possible that the

Fig. 55. Dragon-fly with wings for flapping or vibratory motion
only ; a hovering and darting flight of extreme rapidity.

bird has such control of the air in its bones as to be able thereby
to regulate its ascent and descent in air, much as a fish can
control its movements up and down in water by its swim
bladder. It is certain that the power of flight in birds is much
greater in stormy than in calm weather.

A wide field is open for investigations into this question
of bird flight, and the results might be of great value as well
as of great interest. On page 70 some notes will be found
on the " flight " of flying-fish.

Migration. Occasionally a flock of migrating birds passes

E

over a ship at sea. To some extent the migratory instinct occurs also among fishes and other animals in quest of suitable climate, food, and breeding-places.

How these creatures find their way across great distances to a certain goal is a mystery. Migrating birds—except penguins—fly at a great height (some at from two to three miles up), and generally by night. In dark and wet weather the birds fly lower, and their cries may be heard as they pass. It may be that the old birds lead the way they have so often gone before ; succeeding generations replacing them in turn as leaders. It is difficult to say whether they learn the route by following it year after year, or know it by inherited instinct. The migrations of penguins and seals are still more puzzling problems, though probably they follow in the tracks of their food-supply in a great measure, when food is the object of their migration.

Fig. 56. Flying-fish with fins capable only of sideway movement suitable for gliding flight ; it cannot flap them. The powerful tail projects fish into the air.

Breeding. Off all coasts practically, sea birds assemble in countless numbers on rocks, islands or sandy wastes to breed. Of late much attention has been directed to the domestic economy, etc., of various colonies of breeding birds, and some very interesting facts have been established (Fig. 57).

Reptiles. Off some tropical coasts, in India and elsewhere, snakes are sometimes seen swimming near the land.

The *Pelamys bicolor*, a small snake seldom more than a yard long, is common in the Indian Ocean. Numbers are seen together at times. Like all seagoing snakes, they are very poisonous. A snake gets caught occasionally in the log-line of a ship.

Turtles are frequently met with in the tropics floating

FIG. 57. Molly Mawks Nesting on Laysan Island (Hawaiian Group).
(By the courtesy of the Hon. Walter Rothschild, F.Z.S.)

on the sea surface. They are caught sometimes by bringing a boat quietly and cautiously alongside the floating turtle, which is then turned suddenly on its back before it has had time to realize the danger and escape it in diving. It is hauled into the boat by its hind flippers.

The *Loggerhead Turtle* is the most commonly met with.

D. W.-B.

FIG. 58.   Hawk's-bill Turtle.

The *Green* or *Edible Turtle* and the *Hawk's-bill Turtle* are sometimes seen, as they get carried occasionally far out to sea. The shell plates of this last one supply the tortoiseshell of commerce.

They only come on shore to lay their eggs. In some places the natives catch turtles by baiting a line with a sucking-fish (Fig. 71),--which attaches itself to the turtle, which is then hauled in.

D. W.-B.

CHAPTER V

FISHES

Of the teeming life of the sea but little is seen by the voyager. A fish noticed near the surface becomes an object of the deepest interest to the passengers of a ship.

For our purpose we may classify fishes under three heads : coast fish, surface fish (including all to a depth of 100 fathoms), and deep-sea fish. There are, amongst these, endless varieties of form. The majority are covered with scales of a more

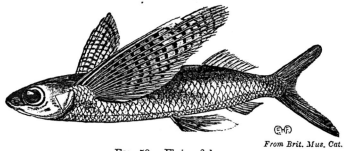

From Brit. Mus. Cat.

FIG. 59.   Flying-fish.

or less horny substance and with a coating of slimy mucus emitted from numerous glands. This slippery substance is of great assistance to the rapid movement of the fish through the water. All fishes breathe through their gills. The lungs common to other animals are replaced in them by an air-sac or swim-bladder, which does not, however, perform any of the functions of a lung, but is rather a lever under the control of the fish which can expand and contract it at will to raise or lower itself in the water.

Flying-fishes are usually first in attracting the attention of voyagers from England to the warmer latitudes where these fishes abound. They are not unlike mackerel and herring in appearance, and a large specimen is about the size of a herring. They have long pectoral fins, not unlike wings when extended, well-developed anal fins, and powerful tails. longer

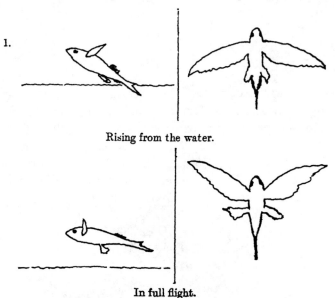

1.

Rising from the water.

In full flight.

FIG. 60.   Flying-fish.

From sketches made by Lieut.-Comdr. Cromie, R.N.

To obtain a fresh impulse the fish comes down onto the water in position 1, and with a rapid movement of the tail and anal fins, obtains a fresh start.

They endeavour to re-enter the water after "flight" with a slight inclination of the head down, but generally they appear to fall back into the water nearly level with it.

and wider at the lower than at the upper half. These fish rise from the sea into the air in shoals, when disturbed by a ship or by an enemy in the sea. Of flight, however, in the sense of bird flight, they are quite incapable.* Their movement in the air is due to propulsion of the powerful tail and their suspension for quite long distances is owing to the support

* The author had notes bearing on the "flight" of the flying-fish in the *Nautical Magazine* for May 1894, and in the *Shipping World*, April 1901.

in the air given by their large pectorals and anal fins. Their air " flight " sometimes extends over 300 yards without touching water. Sometimes the " flight " is just a skimming of the surface as skims a stone in the game " Ducks and Drakes." The fish apparently derives fresh impetus by dipping and vibrating the tail in the sea at intervals. The rise in flight sometimes noticed is nothing more than the blowing up of a gust of wind from a wave, striking the fish from below. If a gust of air should catch the under part of either pectoral fin, the fish is thrown off its course directly, or it falls at once into the water. My observations have been entirely confirmed by the very careful

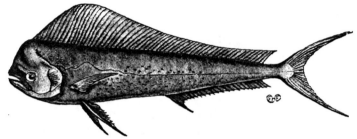

From Brit. Mus. Cat.

FIG. 61. Coryphene.

series of notes and sketches made recently by Lieutenant-Commander Cromie, R.N. The sketches attached are drawn from his notes and sketches. Muscularly, the flying-fish is incapable of any fin-flapping. It may be said to float in air like an aeroplane.

The ship's lights seem powerfully to attract them. They constantly come on board in numbers, at night, and have been captured and kept alive in sea water for some time.

The *Coryphene*, a large and powerful fish, sometimes 6 feet long, is the inveterate foe of the flying-fishes, on which it principally feeds. In sailing-ship days the coryphene was commonly caught and killed for food, as, though not particularly tasty, its flesh was a change from the everlasting salt meat. Curious and beautiful changes occur in the colouring of a dying coryphene. Sailors misname this fish " the dolphin." Other kindred fishes, averaging 5 or 6 feet in length, are the

Albicore and the *Bonito*.   These two were good sport for harpoons or "grains"* on sailing-ship voyages.   The *Tunny*, a fish

FIG. 62.   Catching Bonitos at Sea.

closely allied to the bonito, is seen only occasionally when,
by accident, its pursuit of prey brings it into coastal or shallow

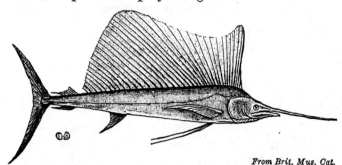

From Brit. Mus. Cat.

FIG. 63.   Sword-fish.

waters.   It is rather good to eat, the cooked fish having a
beef-like flavour.

* A small kind of trident.

A *Sword-fish*, which must not be confounded with the narwhal (p. 39), is sometimes seen. It is a large, powerful and handsome fish, growing to a length of 15 feet, and is capable

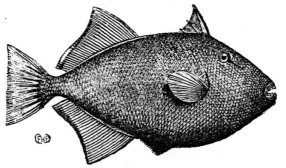

From Brit. Mus. Cat.

FIG. 64. File-fish.

of making leaps out of the water. The " sword " is a prolongation of the upper jaw-bone.

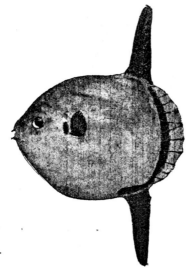

Photo by H. G. Herring

FIG. 65. Rough Sun-fish.

When becalmed in the tropics, or stationary for any reason, a ship may attract the attention of different fishes. The *Surgeon-fish*, for instance, comes round in search of shells and barnacles adhering to the ship's hull. This is a dark fish, with powerful jaws and a tail provided with spurs on each side—formidable fighting weapons, which can inflict nasty wounds. The jaws are hard and strong. Some of the Surgeon-fish family are armed with a strong spine on the fore part of the dorsal fin, instead of with spurs on the tail. Sailors call

From Brit. Mus. Cat.

FIG. 66.   Eagle Ray.

these fishes "Old Maids."   They are easily caught with the lure of a meat bait.

File-fishes have also somewhat similar habits.

Sun-fish are large ungainly creatures, not infrequently seen, especially off the coast of Africa. Flopping about in the water, they appear to swim aimlessly, the head and two long fins only showing at the surface. They are often 8 feet in diameter and may be 500 lb. in weight.

The *Devil-fish*, a species of monster ray, very flat and wide, is occasionally met with. Specimens have been found as large as 18 feet from side to side and up to 1200 lb. in weight.

The characteristics of the *Ray* family are curious. The flat, wide body has a whip-like tail, sometimes armed with dangerous spines—hence the name *Sting Ray*. They are dark coloured and, in spite of their ungainly bulk, are extremely agile in the way of leaping out of the water, but the descent into it is a mighty splash and flop.

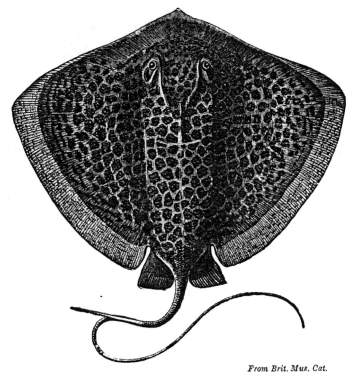

From Brit. Mus. Cat.

FIG. 67.   Sting Ray.

Of all fish—except the flying-fish—the *Shark* is the most frequently seen. Its ugly dorsal fin showing above the water at once attracts attention. More than one seldom appears at a time, and it is usually accompanied by a couple of *Pilot-fish* (Fig. 69), pretty little fellows, whose connexion with their grim companion is hard to understand, though its reality is obvious, and constitutes one of those incongruous natural relationships founded on some system of mutual benefit which we do not under-

stand. War is waged on the shark directly he is sighted. A big
hook baited with some pounds of meat will be lowered over
the stern of a ship in harbour or becalmed at sea. Chain is

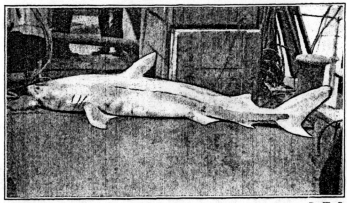

D. W.-B.

Fig. 68. Shark.

used to strengthen the line, which otherwise the shark would
bite through. The hooked shark is hauled on board, a bowline being slipped down over the tail, as the brute fights vigor-
ously for life. A couple of sharp blows on the nose quickly
stun him, and he is then dispatched.* The shark's mouth is
furnished with a perfect battery of powerful teeth. Curious

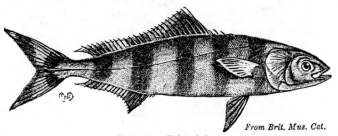

From Brit. Mus. Cat.

Fig. 69. Pilot-fish.

objects are found in its stomach, to which apparently nothing
comes amiss. Frequently a couple of *Sucking-fish* are found
attached to the head of a shark by a disc which is a sort of dorsal

* Very good sport may be had by using a long cod-line and playing the shark
till it is exhausted, when it may be pulled in close to the ship and shot. The line
must be kept clear for running out, and strong gloves are necessary.

fin on the fish's head. The position of the sucking-fish and shark is back to back, and, contrary to the general rule in fish colouring, the back of the sucking-fish is white and the under part (which is uppermost in this case) is dark. These sucking-

Photo furnished by Capt. T. R. Angus.

FIG. 70. Hauling a large Shark on board.

fishes, which attach themselves to other big fish as well as to sharks, vary in length from a few inches to twenty-four or more.

There are numerous varieties of sharks, but those usually seen

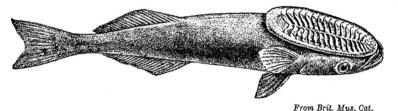

From Brit. Mus. Cat.

FIG. 71. Sucking-fish.

are so alike (with the exception of the *Hammer-headed Shark*) that no one not an expert could recognize the different species. The *Basking Shark* (*Rhinodon*), distinguished by a long dorsal fin, is a monster which may be 50 feet long; and there are other huge varieties, but fortunately those giants have but small teeth and their food consists apparently of the smaller fishes, crustacea, etc. The more savage and voracious sharks vary in length from 6 to perhaps 20 feet. They devour anything and everything that comes in their way. A shark's vitality is extraordinary. The heart, when removed from the body, will continue to beat for a long time. All sharks have tails elongated on the upper lobe. The illustration of the *Hammer-headed Shark* conveys better than words an idea of the curious monster.

D. W.-B.

Fig. 72. Hammer-headed Shark.

The *Thresher* is said to attack whales —*see* p. 38. This is a small but very fierce shark; the upper lobe of its tail is more than usually elongated. It is supposed to beat the sea with its powerful tail to round up a shoal of herring or mackerel, then rushing in amongst them it devours all in its path. The natives in some countries esteem sharks' fins as a delicious diet.

The *Saw-fish* is a monster seldom seen. Its weapon is a long, flat, double-edged spear or saw, projecting

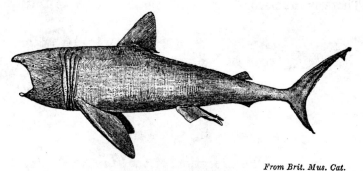

From Brit. Mus. Cat.

Fig. 73. Basking Shark.

from the snout, which would appear to be a particularly useless appendage to a fish. Possibly its function is to tear the flesh by sidelong blows from creatures attacked. Growing to a size of 24 feet, the saw-fish is a formidable foe. One is said to have attacked a man and to have hacked him in two.

In high southern latitudes (between the Cape of Good Hope, the Horn, and Australia) the *Barracouta Fish* may be caught occasionally, by means of a hook baited with a white rag or a bright bit of tin. The barracouta is a splendid swim-

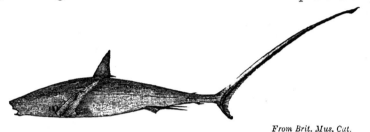

From Brit. Mus. Cat.

FIG. 74. Thresher.

mer, so the speed of a ship is no hindrance to the sport of catching him. But the line must be held out from a steamer's side to clear the propeller. This fish is long and narrow, has a strong jaw and very sharp teeth, and is sometimes 5 feet long, but usually those caught measure from 2 to 3 feet. They are not at all bad to eat.

In the Gulf Weed (fully discussed in the chapter on Sea-weeds) many curious little fishes, *Antennarius*, *Pipe-fishes*, *Sea-horses*, etc., may be caught—strange interesting creatures,

D. W.-B.

FIG. 75. Saw-fish.

which may be kept under observation in a small aquarium or bowl. They are poor swimmers, and keep to the kindly shelter of the weed which they resemble in colouring.

In navigating in coral reefs one comes across *Gar-fish* and *Half-beak*, which rise and leap from the surface after the manner of flying-fish. Sometimes a great commotion occurs among these little fishes when they are invaded by larger foes in quest of capture. The writer has seen the water around his ship alive with them, some jumping right into the boat when harried by a pursuing enemy. The *Gar-fish* (Beline) are long and have long sharp-pointed snouts, and are of a silvery hue. When chased by an enemy they sometimes rise out of the water, the tail only remaining below the surface, which it lashes to and fro.

Sometimes one is lucky enough to see from a ship's deck a shoal of herrings or pilchards on the move, pursued, as a rule, by numerous enemies. It is a curious and beautiful

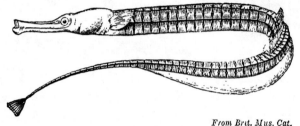

From Brit. Mus. Cat.

Fig. 76.   Pipe-fish.

sight when the shoal appears to rise out of the water, in its flight making what looks like a silver wave on the sea.

The late Frank Buckland has described such a shoal of herrings as being four miles long and two miles wide.

Much might be written of sea fishes and their habits; of their wonderful migrations in quest of food or breeding-places; of the curious forms inhabiting the lower deeps (*see* page 17) and but seldom visible to men. Such matters, however, concern the naturalist rather than the average voyager, who can inform himself from many excellent works, should he feel inclined for more detail than comes within the scope of this volume.

The history of the fisheries of different nations is a fascinating study in economics. There are so many and such different methods of trapping, killing, preparing and preserving this particular branch of the world's food.

Fish congregate sometimes in great masses, especially where hot and cold waters meet. For instance, off the coasts of Chili and Peru, where countless millions of fishes are sometimes seen and may be sailed through for miles.

D. W.-B.

Cuttle " Fish." Some idea of the great cuttle "fish" group is given by the *Octopus*, so often seen in the oddest

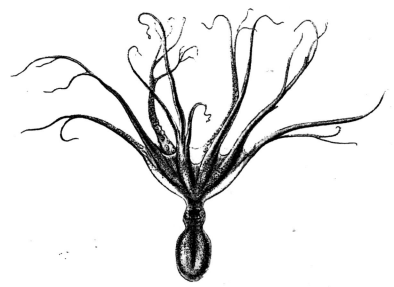

Photo by H. G. Herring.

Fig. 77. Octopus.

positions in aquariums. This creature has a bag-like body, from which protrude eight tentacles fringed with suckers. In the centre of these and of the soft body is a parrot-beak-shaped mouth. Two large eyes are on the outside of the body. Stretching between the tentacles at their base is a mantle or web in which to envelop a prey. In a few species this web extends to the ends of the tentacles. They are dangerous creatures, and men have often been dragged below the surface by them and drowned.

The octopus, however, is not the *Cuttle " Fish "* or *Calamary*,

F

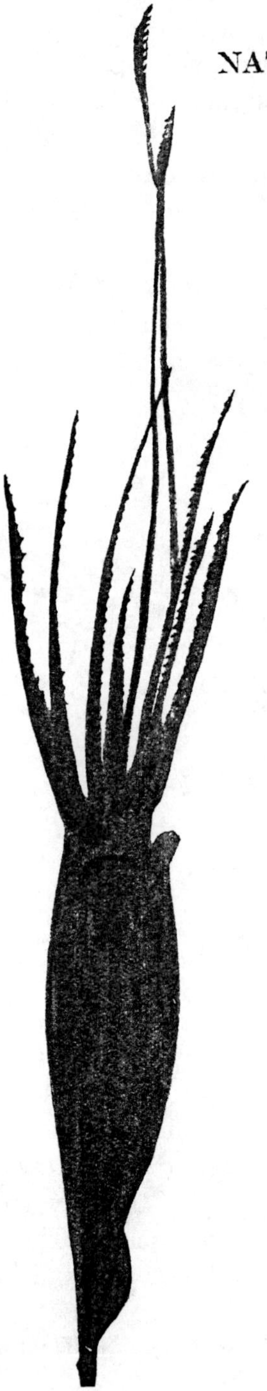

FIG. 78. Giant Squid.

Drawing from photo by H. G. Herring

the latter being a much larger and more formidable creature which has ten tentacles armed with powerful suckers surrounded by horny hooks. Two of these tentacles are of enormous length in comparison with the size of the body.

Small calamaries or *Squids* are sometimes washed on board ships, or they may be drawn up in the suction of the pumps. These may be but a few inches big. The large squids are often monsters 50 feet long. The small varieties are dwellers of the ocean surface. The large ones live in the intermediate depths, where they are preyed on by the sperm whale, which "sounds" to fish for them. Fishes, birds, and animals alike feed with satisfaction on the surface squids; many may be found in the stomach of a captured dolphin.

The mouth of a squid (called squid's beak), of a curious horn-like substance, is in the centre of the body, from which spring the tentacles. These tentacles or arms pass food to the beak, which tears it to pieces.

Shoals of small squids are sometimes met with, and many of them are captured to be eaten,

or used as bait.   The cooked squid is quite good, tasting like
" calf's head."

Practically all the ten-armed squids have a dorsal plate,
called the cuttle-fish bone (commonly used by artists as a
" pen " or eraser).   This bone, just beneath the skin of the back,
apparently supports the soft body.   Some of these curious

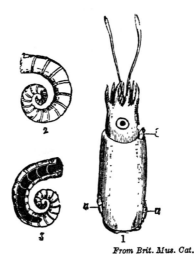

From Brit. Mus. Cat.

FIG. 79.   The Spirula.

1. The animal.   *a.* Portions of the shell exposed in front and
behind.   *b.* The funnel or siphuncle.
2. Side view of shell.
3. Shell in section, to show partitions or septa.

creatures are beautifully coloured, and, like the octopus, they
have the power of more or less adapting their appearance to
their surroundings.

Remarkable but smaller varieties of this family are the
rarely seen *Argonaut* or *Paper Nautilus*, the *Spirula*, and the
Pearly Nautilus.   The shell of the female Argonaut is thin and
delicate.   The male is smaller in size and shell-less.

A living specimen of the Spirula is an extremely rare find,
although the shells abound on many tropical shores.

The *Pearly Nautilus* of both sexes has a substantial shell
interiorly, divided into many chambers or cells.   This is pre-

sumably a deep-sea inhabitant, seldom seen unless captured in a dredge.

Fearful and wonderful are the tales, true and otherwise, told of the cuttle-fish group. Probably the legend of the

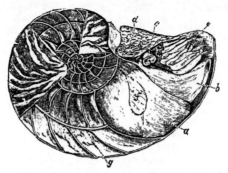

From Brit. Mus. Cat.

Fig. 80.   The Pearly Nautilus.

a. Body ; *b.* Siphuncle ; *c.* Eye ; *d.* Hood ; *e.* Tentacles ; *f.* Muscles of attachment to the shell ; *g.* Siphon.

sea serpent owes its origin to the antics of the gigantic squids, which rise at times to the surface, and in swimming raise parts of their bodies and arms well out of the water.   An encounter with such a monster must be a terrible danger to other dwellers of the sea.   The marks left by their suckers on the tough skins of their whale victors bear witness to the strength of their great tentacles, from whose deadly embrace no smaller creature may escape.   D. W.-B.

CHAPTER VI

PLANT LIFE AND SEA WEEDS

OF all minute forms of plant life at sea the *Diatoms* are the most numerous. In some ocean areas, as the great circum-

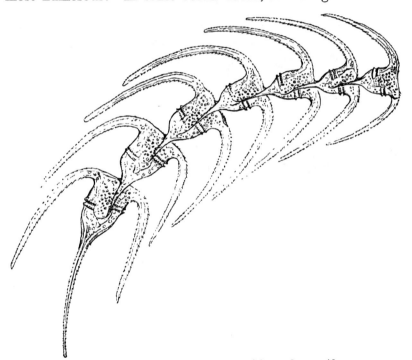

FIG. 81. Peridinium (*Challenger*).   Minute brown Algæ.

polar southern ocean and the northern border of the Pacific, the deposits of dead cases of diatoms have determined the nature of the sea floor. They are of universal distribution, inhabiting fresh as well as salt water. Like the *Radiolarians* the diatoms are minute protoplasmic masses enclosed in flinty or siliceous cases, which are often very beautiful.

A different series of plant life or pelagic algæ includes the *Pyrocystis noctiluca* (so famous for its phosphorescent properties, dealt with elsewhere) and *Trichodesmium*, a weed which, viewed through a lens, resembles a bundle of short stalks.   This minute plant sometimes covers the sea surface like coal dust.

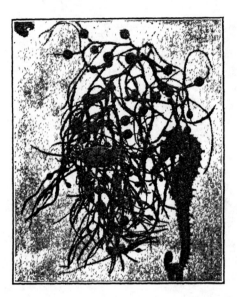

It seems universally distributed, though only sometimes seen in quantities. In log-books it has doubtless often been noted as " dust." It gives a strong smell to the air, and is often called whale's spawn by sailors.

Plankton plant life is at its highest development in the Arctic and in the temperate seas.

Many species of small algæ never come under the notice of ocean travellers. Some varieties bore their way into corals and other growths.

D. W.-B.

FIG. 82.   Gulf Weed, with Sea-horse, Crabs, etc.

The most important in bulk of the true sea-weeds is the Sargassum weed, vast fields of which are in the North Atlantic Ocean and which is found in a less degree in the North Pacific.

In colour this weed is light brown or yellow ; it darkens with age, and becomes covered with a Bryozoan (*Membranifera*). The Sargassum weed bears quantities of large air-vessels containing spores ; it appears in patches, and curiously enough in lines with the wind, so that a ship crosses ribands or bands of it.   Quantities of the weed and its inhabitants may be hauled up in a net attached to a long line if one has the chance of crossing the weed patches in a sailing-ship. With practice one gets expert at throwing and hauling in the net laden with weed full of interesting little animals. Of these the *Antennarius* is the strangest. This queer little fish clings to the weed with armlike fins. It deposits its eggs in a nest, which it makes by building a mass of weed together in sticky gelatinous strings of its own deposit.

Curious small crabs and shrimps inhabit the weed, in which they find protection, as they match it in colour, even to the white markings, which correspond to the white patches of Bryozoan which encrust the weed.

A small naked mollusc and a planarian worm also live on the weed, which itself seems to have been torn from the coasts and islands of Bermuda and of Central America. Supported by its air vessels, it floats for a long time on the surface of the sea; gradually it becomes waterlogged and covered with polyzoa, and finally it sinks into the depths.

Among other sea-weeds, the giant Kelp (*Macrocystis pyrifera*) of the southern ocean is sometimes seen in great rope-like masses covering rocks, and sometimes floating far away from all rocks or land. D. W.-B.

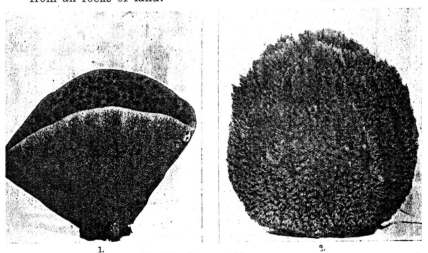

1.   2.

FIG. 83. Commercial Sponges.

1. *Eusponqia officinalis lamella.* 2. *Eusponqia officinalis rotunda.*

CHAPTER VII

CORAL

THE coral reef is such a familiar object in some tropical seas, and the atoll rising from the azure depths is such a remarkable ocean product, that we feel it must not be omitted from the story of the sea.

Sailing through the tropics with the sun behind the ship, and with nothing to break the line of horizon where the blue dome of sky so lightly rests, one may become aware of a strange disturbance in the sea ahead, as if a large school of fish were splashing and playing. With a telescope, however, we perceive that the waves are not haphazard, but are breaking regularly at one place, and that the water near the breakers appears to be of a lighter blue than the surrounding ocean. On going up aloft to gain a better view, we discover that the breakers form a ring around a calm centre, and that here and there a low islet of coral debris exists two or three feet above the sea. Approaching the reef on the lee side, the ship drops anchor on one of the light blue patches, which show a bottom of coral sand, and a boat is lowered to make further investigations. At one point in the ring the breakers seem less formidable and we pull for that spot. The whole reef, except the islets and one or two lumps of dead coral, is just covered, but in the dips between the lines of swell we get some idea of the terrible obstacle to navigation that exists here in the open ocean. We lay on our oars and watch the entrance, if it may be so called. The surf varies in force, and there are intervals when it is comparatively quiet. Selecting one of these, we pull in across the reef as fast as possible.

No language can paint the scene that meets the eye in the clear water under the boat. First the fathomless blue, then some vague outline of a vast steep-sided structure 30 feet below, then a great mass of hidden treasure rising solidly out of the blue, showing caves and corridors of coral rock coated over with delicate forests of fragile trees of all colours. Blue angel-fish paddle slowly through the corridors in the still water

FIG. 84. Margin of Coral Reef. ("Age of the Earth.")

below, parrot-fish almost lie in the coral branches, feeding on parasitical shells, the soft corals and sea-fans bend and rise to each swell, the whole tree-like mass of the reef itself seems to sway as the roller sways over it—and then we are inside, in still water ; and we find ourselves on a quiet shallow lake from which we can watch the ship rolling outside. The lake is rather milky with coral powder from the churn of the swell, and the bottom of it is covered with a somewhat greasy coating of the same. A basking shark is floundering about on the reef, and a turtle passes under the boat.

Mr. Christian's description, in his book " The Caroline

Islands," is so good that we cannot resist quoting it in full.

"As the canoe shoots over the edge of the great coral barrier that looms up through the water like a mighty sea wall sloping down into the deeps, the voyager for the moment feels a novel sensation like that of looking over a giddy precipice. The landward reef-edging bristles with a thousand graceful forms of branching coral and a marvel of submarine algæ; a true garden of the Nereides laid out in gay parterres of oarweed and sea-fan, picked out with scintillating patches of sea-moss of intense electric blue. Nature here deals in odd and whimsical contradictions. Sponge-like corals flourish beside coral-like sponges. On the sandy bottom inshore bask herds of sea cucumbers (Holothurians), black, brown, red, green, and speckled, stretching out their wavy tassels of tentacle to engulf the tiny sea-eels and small fry. Great bright ultra-marine star-fishes lie spread out below, whilst all around on the shelves below the reef-edge sponges are growing in vivid rows and clusters. Sponges grey, sponges green, sponges scarlet as geranium flower, sponges yellow as marigolds, sponges soft, and sponges horny, a goodly sight. Whilst ever and anon comes the rhythmical boom of Ocean's ceaseless thunder rolling on the outer reef and reverberating through the hollow caverns in the honeycombed limestone below; dens where grim and giant poulps and crustacea lurk in the pale green light glimmering deep down below the combing line of surf; where priceless orange cowries stud the debris of the ocean floor like crocuses, living out their little lives far from the reach of conchologist, and shadowed under the ægis of Nature's mightiest forces. We pass over large round table-topped corals of greenish or yellowish brown—each a miniature coral atoll in itself—depressed like a plate in the centre, with raised edges crested by the lip-lipping of the light ripples brimming around their furrowed rims. Hastily we haul our craft high up on the beach of coral sand and dive into the shelter of a palm hut to escape the coming rain storm." . . .

Now, how does this coral reef come here? All around is deep water. On the light blue patch of coral sand, 200 yards from the breakers, there are 30 or 40 feet of water. A short distance farther out, where the colour changes to dark blue, the sounding lead will strike bottom in 15 fathoms (90 feet). Another ship's length out there are 60 fathoms, and if we drop it half a mile out from the reef we may find it goes down to 300 fathoms and then we shall still be touching the slope of a submarine mountain rising from perhaps 1200 fathoms.

It cannot be all coral, for the reef-building coral zooid requires a temperature of about 65° Fahr., and we have seen that that is not found below 100 fathoms and rarely below 60 fathoms.

The great Darwin propounded a theory by which all types of coral reef could be accounted for, viz. by the subsidence of islands. It was known that elevations of coasts and islands had occurred in some localities and subsidence in others. Briefly put, his theory was this. Coral grew on the shores of tropical islands where the temperature favoured its growth, and, growing outwards, formed a Fringing Reef. Then, owing to local contraction of the earth the island settled slowly. The coral zooid built up most rapidly on the outer edge of the reef where it was best supplied with food, and kept up to the sea surface to get the higher temperature.

Thus, in time, as the land settled, a water space arose between the reef and the shore, and a Barrier Reef was formed.

Subsidence still went on, and the islet disappeared beneath the waves, leaving a more or less circular Atoll Reef.

This hypothesis still holds good for areas of subsidence, but it has been found that similar reefs exist where there are areas of elevation.

It may be observed that the strongly indented coast-line of many oceanic islands is a proof of subsidence. Had a long rest or elevation occurred before coral reefs grew up and protected the land, the action of the surf would have tended to shallow up or fill the indentations.

Admiral Sir W. Wharton's theory was that volcanic cones denuded by wave action formed the majority of the foundations on which coral atolls rest. He pointed out that the shelf of shallow water round so many coasts proves that wave action occurs down to 80 fathoms, and the chafing of submarine cables at that depth supports that theory. He also pointed out that the tide extends down to great depths, and that its action is accelerated on meeting such an obstacle as a volcanic cone.

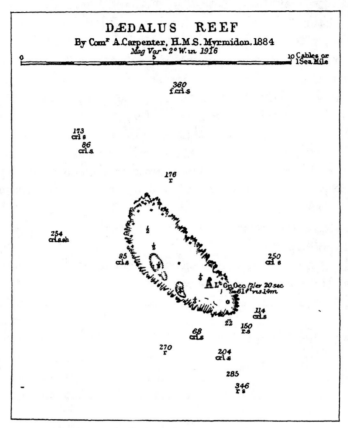

FIG. 85. An Atoll: Red Sea. Soundings in fathoms.

Such cones are always formed of loose material, ashes, scoriæ, etc., and probably the core on cooling would retract considerably. In the later volcanic period of the earth's history many such cones were thrown up. Those on dry land are now mostly worn down, many that were thrown up from the ocean bed to a good height above the surface remain as islands, but others, which only just reached above the sea-

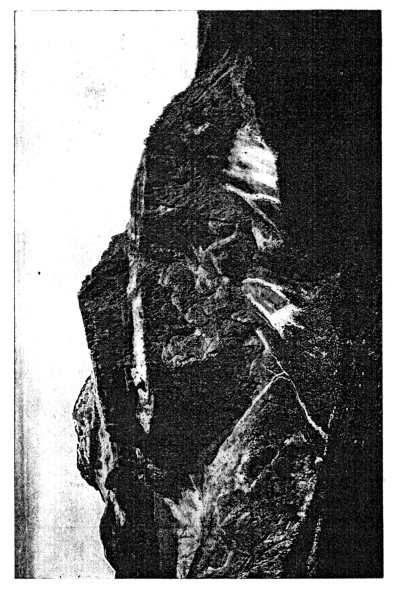

Fig. 86.   A Coral Reef on Mountain top.   The Tyrol.   ("Age of the Earth.")
An Example of Elevation.

surface or perhaps never rose so high, were denuded by wind and wave action lower and lower until in time the encrusting algæ and bottom deposits protected it from further destruction. Then the coral zooid settled on it and built its way up.

The coral zooid belongs to the class of Actinozoa and is therefore related to the sea anemone. The embryo is a little free-swimming body which is carried along by currents until it meets with something hard to which it can attach itself and grow into a coral tree. Under suitable conditions of clean water and high temperature, the little embryos attach themselves, bud, grow, spread into a patch, and the colony is increased and helped by a similar growth of Hydrocorallinæ and Alcyonidæ. As it climbs upward, towards the higher temperature and the greater surface food-supply, the first settlers become smothered out and consolidated into calcareous coral rock. The sea holds all minerals in suspension to a more or less degree, and the condition in which lime is held is such that many animals can extract and secrete it from the water. When, however, it is once extracted and secreted it becomes under ordinary conditions insoluble. The coral zooid secretes the lime and the coral skeleton spreads over large areas, chiefly as an encrustation.

Owing to the tides the outer edge of the patch gets the most food and the coral there grows the fastest. Where ocean currents obliterate the more sluggish tides one side of the colony is favoured more than the other, and a crescent-shaped reef arises to the surface.

On reaching the surface a fresh action comes into play, that of the breakers. Coral grows strongest on the side of the prevailing wind and sea, but the branches being delicate are constantly torn off and hurled toward the centre of the patch, where they tend to smother first those zooids which are already weakening owing to scarcity of food. From the greasy feeling of dead coral under water it seems that it suffers some dissolution in sea water, and the boring shells and algæ, and the coral-eating fish, assist in reducing it to fragments. Feeders on coral sand, such as the Holothurians, grind what is left into fine particles that are swept away by the currents. Hence a steady destruction goes on of what was once the centre of the living colony, and with the destruction a slight deepening which results in the lagoon already described.

Mr. Wood-Jones, who spent fifteen months on Coco-Keeling Atoll, is of opinion that atoll lagoons do not deepen, but get shallower. He considers that the atoll form comes about from the prevailing wind and sea striking the reef chiefly from one direction. This results in the broken debris being carried round on either side in two horns on which more coral settles and grows to the surface ; and, the process being continued, the horns at length meet in a circle, or an ellipse. As a support to this theory he observes that coral islets formed on a reef always adopt the crescent shape, the convex side being to the surf. He considers that silt is alone the factor that prevents the central portion of the atoll from growing, but he seems to have missed the scouring of the fine silt from off the atoll that takes place and so prevents filling up.

As the ocean swell mounts and swirls across the reef, the centre lagoon becomes too full and there is a constant discharge neutralizing the inflow. Submerged coral banks are commonly of a circular or oval shape similar to that of atolls, and it is difficult to say whether they have subsided or whether they are rising to the surface.

Should the surf be very high so much broken coral may be thrown up as to form a small islet, and this tends to grow by additions. Sea-gulls and migrating birds will now rest on it, and they drop guano, and possibly some seeds which have clung to their leg feathers. Floating sea-weed and drift-wood will be stranded, which, rotting in the tropical sun, will help to form a soil. Crabs and shell fish make their homes on it and carry seeds, such as those of mangrove and Pandanus, into their burrows. A heavier storm than usual may block the burrows, and the buried seed will develop and form a shrub. So the little coral islet in time becomes green. One day a cocoa-nut, floating from another islet, is thrown on it and buried, and the reef is no longer a danger to mariners, for it becomes marked by a grove of palms.

It is not necessary that volcanic ash should be the material of the foundation. A crinkle or fold of the sea bottom may be pushed up by contraction of the earth, and, if this is of a friable nature, it is first worn down, then consolidated by the

FIG. 87.   A Coral Island Forest.   ("Age of the Earth.")

growth of encrusting algæ, then built upon, and a chain of coral reefs is formed, such as the Maldives and Laccadives. The great Barrier Reef of Australia, 1000 miles long, is so straight that it may have risen from a ridge of elevation. All over the tropics there are submerged coral reefs, such as the Macclesfield Bank in the China Sea and the Pedro Bank off Jamaica, both of which the writer surveyed. On the first he found the coral growing strongly all around the outer rim, which rose to within 50 or 60 feet of the surface; and also growing, but less strongly, in the centre of the bank, which was submerged 240 feet.

On the Pedro Bank there were a few coral islets, and one rock, on the edge facing the prevailing wind and current, but all the rest was submerged from 80 to 115 feet.

From the boat in which we have just crossed the reef into the calm lagoon, we can now get out and walk about on the inside portion of the great ring. Although the coral here is blunted, a good pair of boots is a necessity, for the antlers are pointed and sea-eggs have nasty spines. What a floral fairy-land it is. You almost fear to crush so much beauty. There

From Brit. Mus Cat.

FIG. 88. Coral. *Stylaster flabelliformis* (½ nat. size).

are golden and sapphire tipped antlers of Madrepores, bunches of ruby organ-pipe Tubipore, amber-tinted brainstones, mauve-coloured vases, bouquets of Galaxea, fleshy corallines, and mushroom-shaped Fungias. Purple masses of sea-fan are rising and falling with the swell, which sends its impulses through all the channels between the coral heads. The little polyps or zooids are showing their tentacles, and this gives colour to the growth. They have lasso-like stinging threads

.G

with which to capture the microscopic life already described. Each coral tree is a colony in itself where all the individuals collect food for the sustenance of the whole, and each secretes a part of the corallum. Half buried in the reef one may see the shells of giant clams (Tridacnidæ) weighing a hundred pounds. Woe betide you if you put your foot into one. The shells close with an iron grip and crush your foot, and only a pickaxe will release you. As you move over the reef and your shadow falls on them the little polyps retreat and the bejewelled branches look dead.

D. W.-B.

FIG. 89.   Breakwater on Coral-encrusted Reef at Pernambuco.*

At low water spring tides large portions of reef are temporarily uncovered, but coral will not die under five or six hours exposure to the air.

I have said that the reef is ever growing outwards, and this makes it overhang, and ever and again a large piece too heavy to be flung inwards is snapped off and sinks on to the slope of the foundation of the reef; when broken coral falls into clean water, it continues to grow and to multiply, and so it soon consolidates to the slope. The blocks that fall too deep are killed by the low temperature, but in time they form a talus that mounts up to the reef-building zone, and thus the

* See *Science Gossip* for June 1890 for an account of this reef by Capt. Wilson-Barker.

reef extends. The calcareous algæ bind the blocks together as firm and as strong as the coral, and they thrive in strong currents and surf. An interesting example of their cementing agency is shown in the consolidation of the reef which forms the natural breakwater of Pernambuco. Owing to the conflict between the outflow of the rivers and the easterly winds and seas, the river silt has settled in long lines a short distance

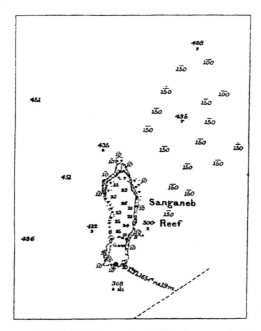

FIG. 90. Sanganeb Reef, Red Sea. An Atoll. Commander Carpenter, 1884.
Soundings in fathoms. (Scale about 1 inch to 2½ miles.)

off the coast and parallel to it. This loose deposit of silt has been so firmly bound together by calcareous algæ that it is now as solid as rock and forms a site for much beautiful marine growth. H. de V. Stacpoole describes a coral reef as " A living land that repairs itself, when injured, by vital processes, and resists the eternal attack of the sea by vital force."

As the combing swell expands its force over the reef and discharges over the lowest part of the reef into the ocean, carrying with it the silt with which it has become clouded, the growing coral in the channel of discharge is to some extent smothered and killed. Hence there is formed on every atoll, generally at the side opposite the prevailing wind, a passage way for boats. Better marked passage ways, frequently available

Fig. 91. Lophohelia. A Deep-sea Coral.

for ships, are found on barrier reefs opposite some valley of the neighbouring island down which streams run and discharge their silt.

In the fine aquarium at Naples living corals and corallines may be seen with their polyps showing. Some very beautiful Medusæ may often be studied there too, but these ocean butter-flies are with difficulty kept long in captivity.

Coral reefs are only found between latitude 30° N. and

latitude 30° S. where the surface temperature does not fall below 65°. Where colder waters well up from below towards the surface, or where the sea is muddy with the discharge of rivers, reef coral will not grow ; and it is not found on either coast of South America south of latitude 10° N. nor on the west coasts of Africa or North America.

One of the most interesting duties of the naval surveyor is the fixing the position geographically of coral islets and atolls.

FIG. 92. Flabellum. A Deep-sea Coral.

When practicable he carries this out by landing on them and taking observations of the stars. The writer landed with a companion on the Morant Cays, off Jamaica, for this purpose at 6 P.M.; and at 2 A.M., having secured good observations, the two observers stretched themselves out on the lee side of the islet for a few hours sleep.

The surf was thundering on the reef to windward, and the rich ozone filled their lungs and made them more disposed to run a race than sleep. The frigate birds and the booby gulls were resting on the low shrubs, and their chatter also kept sleep away. At last after long waiting sleep came, and they lay still. Then suddenly the writer found himself wide awake, for his hair had been pulled ! Considering that they were on a small sandy islet out of sight of land this came as a surprise, and he sat up and looked around. His companion was asleep, ripples of water broke silently near their feet, the surf thundered in the distance, and the stars looked quietly down. He felt he had been dreaming, and so laid down again. Then he felt his coat pulled ! Sitting up quickly he whisked round expecting to see . . . he knew not what. All was still; a few lumps of broken coral lay about, and the ship's light showed as she rolled at anchor outside, but there was nothing moving. Then he dissembled and lay down again facing the other way, and kept his eyes open. And then the lumps, that had appeared to be dead coral, raised themselves and sidled towards him. They were crabs, and they had doubtless taken us to be drowned mariners, and expected a good meal !

A. C.

CHAPTER VIII

SURFACE LIFE AND OCEAN DEPOSITS

HAVING now written much about the depths of the sea, let us come back to the surface, for after all it was at or near the surface that discoveries were made by the *Challenger* which led to greater results than were obtained by research lower down. If you take an ordinary muslin bag like a butterfly net and tow it astern of a boat or slow-moving ship for a quarter of an hour, then reverse it into a bowl of clean sea water, you will be surprised to find the bowl teeming with minute creatures darting hither and thither, gleaming and scintillating with opalescent colours. Under a microscope or good pocket lens magnifying some twenty diameters, hundreds of little shrimp-like forms will be seen, strange looking larvæ of fish and of crustaceans, and rapidly moving shapes of animated jelly.

With a higher power, say sixty diameters, new forms will appear—Globigerina, Orbulina, and other Foraminifera, smaller larvæ, minute Sponges, Rotifera, and Infusoria. With a yet higher power we begin to trace the patterns and structure of the Radiolarians, that can only be compared in beauty with snow crystals. And under a yet higher power, say 250, we are able to pick out the Diatoms, those minute cells of plant life that pervade all water.

In cold seas the surface is sometimes rendered opaque and of a dull red colour by the large amount of this minute life, and, strange as it may appear, the great whale and other large fish subsist to a great extent on them ; indeed their

103

stomachs are sometimes found to be crammed with them to such an extent that the mass has to be dug out with a spade.

It has been suggested that shipwrecked sailors adrift on a raft would not suffer from starvation if they were provided with one or two tow-nets, and it has been seriously proposed to start a potted shrimp company and employ a vessel to catch these Plankton.

The Prince of Monaco used a net ten yards in width, having wide open wings, a silk body of finer mesh, and a bottom of the finest silk gauze. He tells us that in the intestine of a single sardine he found about twenty million Peridiniæ, which is one of the Infusoria. Some of the microscopic life is so small that it passes through the meshes, and the *Michael Sars* made use of a whirling machine that whirled tubes of sea water round until all the organisms in them were driven to the end of the tubes. They could then be removed and placed under the microscope.

The small crustaceans such as Copepods, in appearance like tiny shrimps, are the most widely spread and prolific group of the whole animal kingdom, but the Globigerina seem to out-number any other organism on the face of the earth. They are Rhizopods, having a spiny calcareous case or shell which is perforated with holes, through which the body itself can be protruded as flexible filaments.

There are larger species in warm waters than in cold, and their remains form the greater part of marine deposits now forming, and probably make up the larger part of all the geological sedimentary formations found on dry land.

The Radiolarians, small as they are, have little plants (unicellular algæ) growing on them parasitically in the form of bright yellow cells. The plants seem to grow on the Radio-larians and the latter to feed on the plants, a somewhat re-markable accommodation. In their turn the Radiolarians and other Protozoa form the universal food of deep-sea life.

Nothing can approach the wonder and beauty of these forms. They may perhaps be likened to snow crystals ; but the latter are limited to certain types of design, whereas the Radiolarians are of all shapes and patterns.   From the *Challenger's* deepest sounding, 4475 fathoms, only a very small quantity of mud was raised, but in it were the remains of 338 different species.

Trichodesmium, dealt with in Chapter VI, is a notable form of minute plant found on the surface, and the Coccospheres and Rhabdospheres are still more minute plant-like forms found at all depths in tropical and subtropical waters.

Millions of these beautiful forms are thrown ashore every few seconds by waves beating on our coasts.   As the wave runs up the shingle or sand beach you will notice that the tip of the wave does not return, but sinks into the beach.   As it sinks the little organisms are left, and it is possible when the tide is falling to collect them, with some of the fine sand, and put them under the microscope.

Well, these birds and butterflies of the ocean are all transparent, and under magnifying power you can watch their internal circulation, their muscles working, their food digesting, and so on.   You can see them lay eggs and you can see the eggs hatch out, or the young develop in the capsule.   Many of them are very fierce looking and have powerful jaws for their size, or are defended by numerous spines.   The jelly-like forms are the most wonderful, shaped like delicate bells or globes or mushrooms.   They either move by opening and shutting like an umbrella, or by waving small hairs called cilia, which are so fine that they are not easily seen.

This is the living side of the picture—the whole sea is full of minute life, but chiefly near the surface.   What happens when these tiny organisms die ?   So far as we know they are not long lived, so there must be a continuous rain of their dead bodies to the bottom.   On the way down no doubt many are eaten, and some are eaten at the bottom.   Under that great pressure and in that low temperature decomposition acts but slowly, and the deep-sea bottom life eats all that comes to it.

Yet numbers must reach the bottom and get covered up by

others before they can be eaten or dissolved, for it is found that the deposits are composed almost entirely of their remains.

As they sink slowly down, the flesh and beautiful spines fall off under the attacks of acids in the water, the organic tissue is replaced by carbonate and phosphate of lime, and the wonderful little microscopic structure is replaced by a plaster cast. Sometimes it is an outer cast that we find, sometimes an inner. Sometimes the coating is of green or blue mud, if near a continent, and then a glauconitic cast is formed. This

FIG. 93. Globigerina Ooze (*magnified*) with finer amorphous particles washed away.

occurs chiefly in shallow waters down to 500 fathoms, for in such depths there is a considerable accumulation of terrigenous matter, dead leaves, twigs, and river mud, glauconite being formed by a combination of potassium salts and silicates of alumina in the presence of organic matter.

Sir John Murray points out that owing to the viscosity of sea water, which depends on its temperature, the sinking is more rapid in warm than in cold waters and therefore more rapid in the upper layers than in the lower. Many of the Diatoms and other Plankton vary their form in order to adapt their floating power to the varying conditions of viscosity.

Between 500 and 1700 fathoms the deposit that thus forms on the bottom is generally white, consisting principally of carbonate of lime. From 1700 fathoms down to the greatest depths these muds gradually lose their white appearance and become more and more tinged with red, a colour formed by oxide of iron. Below 3000 fathoms it becomes of a chocolate colour owing to the presence of oxide of manganese.

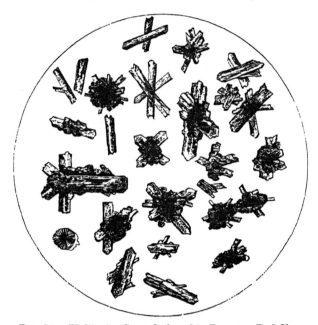

FIG. 94.   Phillipsite Crystals found in Deep-sea Red Clay.

Mixed with the mud at all depths, but specially noticeable in very deep soundings, are volcanic particles which have either been thrown up under water, or have floated through the air from distant volcanoes, or have come from the stellar regions in the form of cosmic dust. Hence the presence of iron and manganese. Red clay, however, may be formed also by the chemical decomposition of rocks at the bottom which, owing to the protection of the ocean, have not been overlaid by gravels and sands.

The amount of free carbonic acid in the sea increases with

the depth and eventually dissolves the delicate shells of Globigerina ooze. It has less power over the siliceous skeletons of Radiolaria and Diatoms, and so where these fill the surface waters there are large deposits of their remains at the bottom (*see* Fig. 96), all the more evident owing to the dissolution of the Foraminifera. In the great depths, where Radiolarians and Diatoms do not happen to be present in quantity, the volcanic and meteoric residue forms the chief element. Peroxide of manganese will collect and concrete round any hard nucleus; and in the Pacific, where there are large areas of depths of about 3000 fathoms, the *Challenger* frequently dredged up hundreds of manganese nodules from the size of a marble to that of a man's fist (*see* Fig. 6, p. 19). These contained as a nucleus hard objects such as the ear-bones of whales, sharks' teeth, pumice stone, etc. It is apparent that the deposit in great depths must be very slow indeed, as it was not unusual to dredge up sharks' teeth of a species known to be long extinct.

Owing to the non-dissolution of the Foraminifera in depths under 1500 or 1700 fathoms before they get covered up, the deposit in lesser depths must be much more rapid than in the greater.

Telegraph engineers think there is reason for supposing that in the North Atlantic about one inch of Globigerina Ooze accumulated at 1700 fathoms in nine years.

The sounding tube brings up sections of the bottom deposit, and in shallow waters it is found that the casts of the lower shells are still entire owing to being covered. Thus comparatively shallow depths tend to become more shallow quickly.

The German Antarctic Expedition in 1901 obtained some good sections of bottom muds. In 3950 fathoms near the equator, in the Atlantic, they brought up a section eighteen inches deep. The uppermost six inches consisted of Red Clay with numerous fragments of volcanic rock. Then followed four bands of different colour passing from brownish grey to dark, and then to light grey. The dark grey layer resembled a terrigenous deposit; and the light grey, the lowest, was the only one containing any proportion of calcium carbonate. This looks as if, in the course of ages, there had been a gradual deepening at that spot. Off the Cape of Good Hope they brought up from 2750 fathoms a section of mud twenty-four inches deep. The upper four and a half inches consisted of a brown clayey quartz-sand with very little volcanic or calcareous material, while the next five inches were almost pure Globigerina Ooze with fragments of the upper layer. The lower part consisted of material similar to the upper layer, but with less sand. All this indicates considerable changes of level; yet, as we have before remarked, the main outlines of continents are considered to have remained unchanged since Palæozoic times.

The Atlantic has more terrestrial matter flowing into it from rivers, and from the Mediterranean, than the Pacific has; and the drift of wind-blown sand from the Sahara is also a factor.

In depths of less than 1000 fathoms we find very varied formations. Off a large river the bottom material is largely composed of decaying vegetable matter and fine mineral particles, which, mixed with the Foraminifera, forms a mud called, geologically, Green Sand. If the coast consists of chalk cliffs a white amorphous mud is formed, caused by the wearing away of the cliffs. Off a coral reef the deposit chiefly consists of fine particles of coral powdered by the thundering surf. Off volcanic coasts, as Mexico, Japan, and Sumatra, volcanic sands occur near the coast, and volcanic muds farther out.

The various muds have either been named after the organisms that form their chief constituent, or after the colour. Thus we have " Green Mud," " Pteropod Ooze," " Globigerina Ooze," " Red Clay," " Radiolarian Ooze," " Diatom Ooze," " Chocolate Mud."

The Pteropods are minute free-swimming molluscs which have very thin calcareous shells that dissolve at about 1200 fathoms. With the Copepods they discolour the water for miles and form a staple diet for whales. Their remains are generally found on the oceanic ridges and near coral reefs in the warmer seas.

Radiolarians and Diatoms build up their structures by abstracting silica from the ocean water. During life this

FIG. 95. Radiolarian Ooze.
(*Highly magnified*)

is protected from dissolution by the admixture of albuminoid matter, but after death the silica is gradually dissolved. Thus from time to time a considerable amount of free silica is present in the depths. It has been suggested that when the water becomes overcharged the free silica seizes on forms such as sponges, sea-eggs, and shells, and forms nodules that we call flints. Flints showing the form and impression of such bottom life are quite common. It does not appear to be necessary that there should be a nucleus, as is the case with the manganese nodule, and one may often find a fossil sea-egg (or urchin) that is simply black flint throughout. Owing, however, to the fact that flint slabs are found in chalk fissures, where it must have formed after the chalk was elevated above the sea, the above theory may require modification. It must be observed that flints have never been dredged.

FIG. 96. Diatom Ooze.
(*Highly magnified*)

The fine mud of rivers and surf-beaten coasts only settles in depths beyond wave action, say 80 fathoms; and this depth, generally called the 100-fathom line, is pretty well marked on all our charts.

The Holothurians and Echinoderms, the most abundant of

the bottom-living deep-sea animals of any size, have their intestines crammed with the material of the deposit on which they are captured. The Holothurian captures the small organisms on its tentacles and draws them into its sack-like body.

It will be readily seen that this rain of dead organisms will gradually eliminate all irregularities of the ocean floor, just as a heavy fall of snow eliminates the furrows of a ploughed field.

Hence rocks and stones are never found in depths over 300 fathoms except where some wandering ice-berg in high latitudes has dropped its glacier-borne rock. The ocean floor is practically a smooth plain.

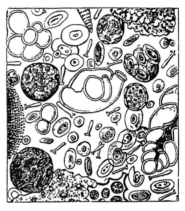

Now it was the recognition of these great ocean deposits, and of the important part that they play in the geology of the earth's sur-face, that was the greatest result of the *Challenger* expedition.

The beautiful chalk downs of the south-east of England have by earth movements been pushed

Fig. 97.   Minute Calcareous particles.
Globigerina Ooze.
(*Magnified*)

up from the deep sea, having formed there as a *deposit* very similar in constituents to Globigerina Ooze.

Of course the pressure and consolidation that it has under-gone has crushed the individual forms into a paste; but if a piece of this chalk is well soaked in water, lightly crushed, and stirred until a good milky deposit settles to the bottom of the glass, then this deposit, put under the microscope, will reveal the crushed fragments of Foraminifera, Radiolarians, Diatoms, and Sponge spicules. Many thousands of years have passed since the chalk in the downs was formed. In northern Iceland the lava and ash ejected in the volcanic age spread over the chalk that was already there.

Similarly the Oolite of Gloucester and Somerset, the Green

Sands of Surrey and Hampshire. the Carboniferous Limestone of Derbyshire, the Coral Sands of the Jura mountains,
and many other geological formations, are entirely composed
of ocean life, and were therefore once ocean deposits. The
method of reducing a piece of rock to the thinness of a wafer
and then observing its structure by transmitted light led to
the discovery that they often contained the complete delicate

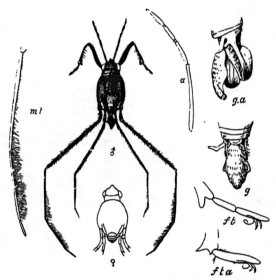

FIG. 98. Halobates, a Pelagic Insect (*Challenger*).

skeletons of minute pelagic life, showing that in those cases
the rock was formed from ocean muds *in situ*.

Pelagic animals which have the power of distending or
contracting and thus rising in the water or falling do so
probably for these reasons, viz. :

Diurnally, to get a change of light or temperature.

Occasionally, on account of boisterous weather.

Seasonally, for unknown reasons, probably physical.

Large fresh-water lakes, like the ocean, have each their
regular shore fauna, a deep-water fauna, and a pelagic fauna.

Globigerina Ooze covers about 50,000,000 square miles of the
sea bottom ; Red Clay 51,500,000 ; Diatom Ooze 11,000,000 ;

Blue Mud 14,500,000; Radiolarian Ooze 2,250,000; Coral Mud 2,750,000; Green Mud 1,000,000; Volcanic Mud 750,000; Pteropod Ooze under 500,000.

This is the microscopic life of the ocean under-world, the existence of which was hardly suspected a century ago. Hidden beneath the waves, out of our range of vision, it has yet been there from time immemorial; indeed it is probable that it pre-ceded life upon land. Hitherto man's knowledge of living creatures has depended chiefly on his need to make use of them for his own purposes, or for their removal from this sphere if inimical to his welfare. Through a growing love of scientific research this under-world has now been entered and fresh discoveries every year reveal how our globe is peopled by marvellous forms of which we had no conception.

A. C.

PLANKTON FAUNA

Reference has been made in Chapters II and VI to the Medusæ, the butterfly jellies of the ocean. Besides the common umbrella forms, varying in size from half an inch diameter to three feet across, so commonly met with, there are many that can be seen at or close to the surface in fine weather. Of these perhaps the most common is "Physalia," the "Portuguese man-of-war," so called by our bluejackets because they are frequently met with off the coast of Portugal, which is a country that does not possess a fleet. It has a swimming bladder about four inches long, coloured like a rainbow and shaped like a Noah's Ark, and below that a bunch of polypites and some long blue transparent stinging tentacles. The latter are not visible in the blue water, but are capable of paralysing small life that becomes entangled in them.

The Velella is a silvery disc about the size of a florin, having erected on it a stiff sail of a semicircular form. Underneath is a single polypite and numbers of blue tentacles. It is a difficult object to see as it looks like a drop of foam, but they are sometimes seen in large numbers in the tropics.

H

The Ianthina, a violet coloured snail with a very delicate shell belonging to the order Gasteropoda, is sometimes met with in great numbers. It is able to inflate a delicate membrane which acts as a float; and it is this float, having the appearance of a group of small soap bubbles, that shines white on the water and catches the eye. When annoyed, Ianthina discharges a purple cloud and rapidly sinks. The Romans collected these Gasteropods and used the purple fluid as a dye.

The Salpæ, tube-like transparent jellies belonging to the Tunicates, are remarkable in being seen sometimes in long chains, or in groups, or as single individuals. They progress by contractions and dilatations of the tubular body, and are generally luminous at night when disturbed. They will be always seen in warm climates when the sea is calm and the ship at rest.

The Ctenophora resemble the Salpæ, but are more highly organized, and they progress by small hairs (cilia) which outline their bodies. Some forms elongate to a flat ribbon shape 3 or 4 feet in length.

The Barnacle or " Acorn Shell " is frequently found adhering to floating wood, the backs of whales, and the bottoms of ships; it is sometimes found floating in clusters of its own kind with or without a nucleus, so that it may almost be reckoned among the Plankton. It belongs to the group Cirripedia, and is allied to the crabs; but early in life, after some remarkable metamorphoses, it attaches itself by the head to some object, forms a multivalve shell, and develops feather-like feet with which it passes water and food to its mouth.

.A. C.

CHAPTER IX

LIGHT AND PHOSPHORESCENCE

"Beyond the shadow of the ship
    I watched the water snakes.
They moved in tracks of shining white;
And when they reared, the elfish light
    Fell off in hoary flakes.

"Within the shadow of the ship
    I watched their rich attire:
Blue, glossy green and velvet black
They coiled and swam, and every track
    Was a flash of golden fire."
                    The Ancient Mariner.

WHEN the sun is low most of its rays are reflected and do not
enter the water, but when it is high they penetrate freely
to considerable depths. Captain Wilson-Barker is of
opinion that just as the light waves of an invisible star im-
print themselves on a photographic plate after many hours of
exposure, so, possibly, the solar light waves would be found,
if a long enough exposure could be made, to reach the pro-
foundest depths.

The *Michael Sars* in 1910 found by experiment that there
is a good deal of light at 500 fathoms, but that plates are un-
affected at 800 fathoms after two hours exposure.

On entering the water, light rays are bent toward the per-
pendicular, and break up into the usual spectrum colours.
The dispersion, however, is not great, and actual white light may
be said to penetrate to 50 fathoms. The ultra-red rays are
absorbed by the uppermost layers, the red rays are weakening
at 50 fathoms; at 250 fathoms only the blue and ultra-violet

rays are found, but they are still fairly strong at that depth.

Although darkness may be said to reign supreme below 700 fathoms, so far as the light of the sun goes, there is very little doubt that the depths are fairly well lit up with a phosphorescent glow which enables organisms to make use of their eyes or light organs.

The whole question of light and vision in the great depths is as yet imperfectly understood, and we can only, by marshalling certain facts together, let the reader form his own opinion of the conditions that exist down below. Near the surface animals are dark or deep blue looked at from above, bright and silvery looked at from below. At the surface they are mostly transparent, but in deep water where there is no sunlight they are dark. It is difficult to be certain whether this is protective colouring or not; it certainly looks so. There is undoubted protection colouring of marine life special to certain surroundings, as among those that inhabit patches of Gulf weed or coral reefs. The colouring of deep-sea creatures is very marked. Shrimps and prawns caught in shallow waters are the colour of the sand and only turn red on being boiled, but the deep-sea crustacean is generally a bright red. Below the limit of the red rays probably a red crustacean is but dimly visible. From above, the sea appears to us to be blue on a fine day ; but under water to 50 fathoms everything is under a gradually darkening green light.

The eyes of fishes and crustaceans decrease in size as the depth at which they are found increases, but there are exceptions to this rule. Some have only rudimentary eyes, and there appears to be a depth, 250 fathoms, below which imperfect organs of vision are common. Many fish and crustaceans are quite blind, but these are generally furnished with long feelers, or possibly possess a sense which informs them of the presence of danger or food. The discovery of reflectors and lenses in the light organs of pelagic life seems to show that these organs serve the function of projecting light in definite directions.

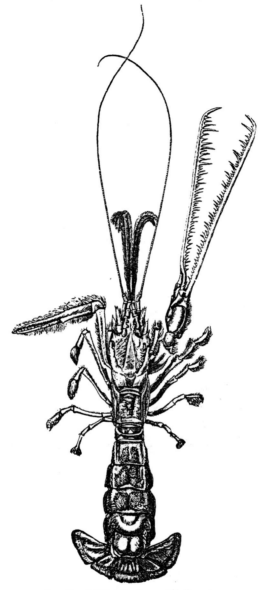

Fig. 99.   A Blind Crustacean (*Challenger*).

Deep-sea fishes appear to be day blind—that is to say, their eyes are not sensitive to daylight, yet they appear to be of use. The probability is that they are sensitive to phosphorescent light. Such light is known to be produced freely in salt water by a great many organisms. The Alcyonarians or fleshy corals, comprising all the sea-fans and sea-pens, cover considerable areas of the bottom in moderately deep water, and, being phosphorescent, give large fields of bluish light in which animals with light organs would see clearly. Then there are immense numbers of Medusæ and Salpæ of all descriptions that can emit the light, and one of the most beautiful sights in the writer's memory was the lighting up of the *Challenger's* sails as she rose and fell in a tropical sea. A very slight irritation is sufficient to cause these delicate organisms to emit the light, even an approaching shower of rain will be marked by a phosphorescent line, and, as every sailor knows, it is not uncommon when pulling a ship's boat in some tropical harbour on a dark night to see phosphorescent gems sparkling on the blade of every oar.

It is probable, however, that the main part of these surface exhibitions is caused by various kinds of bacteria, millions of which could lie on a penny. They are colourless rod-like bodies, some of which are known to be capable of movement by cilia. They multiply and develop at an enormous rate, and only require suitable food and the presence of oxygen to bring out their fires.

Captain Wilson-Barker on several occasions noticed that when the sea was covered with oily patches and streaks visible in daylight, much phosphorescence would be seen after dark ; and it is possible, as he pointed out in a paper read in 1906 before the *Challenger* Society, that this oiliness—perhaps the product of some decaying fish—was full of bacteria which gave out light. The writer has seen the Red Sea by day looking as if covered by floating reddish sand. On collection it was found to be made up of countless numbers of Noctiluca, a small jelly about the size of a pin's head. Each jelly had an orange-red central spot which after dark emitted phosphorescent light. Thousands of tons of Noctiluca are sometimes washed on shore in the Red Sea, and the beach appears covered with piles of blood. When fish find themselves in one of these brilliant swarms they seem to go quite mad.

On one occasion, near the Azores, a large colony of Pyrosoma came up in the *Challenger* trawl congregated as a single large jelly, 4 feet by 1 foot. This was so phosphorescent at night that by the mere pressure of a finger we could write our names over it in letters of passing fire.

As many of the most minute forms of life are phosphorescent, and as the surface teems with these, one sometimes gets extraordinary effects. There is a phenomenon called " The White Sea " when, from some unknown cause, every one of the light producers seems to be actively at work. The atmosphere seems to reflect it, and the mariner finds himself in a luminous fog which obliterates the horizon and induces a sense of insecurity. Ski-ists sometimes find themselves in the same difficulty on large stretches of pure white snow which give no indication, owing to the absence of shadow, of sudden depressions. Both in the Gulf of Aden and in the Persian Gulf some remarkable displays have been reported. Mr. Hoseason of the S.S. *Kilwa* reported in 1900–01, in the entrance to the Persian Gulf, and also off the delta of the river Indus, that he saw remarkable concentric rings of phosphorescence. These appeared to spread out at an enormous speed, calculated at about 30 miles a minute, which gave the sea something of the appearance of a field of corn swept over by a strong breeze. The area covered by the display was roughly 50 miles, and the sparkles had the look of something being dropped into the water. Some of the water was collected, but nothing visible to the naked eye was found in it. (*See Journal of the R. Meteorological Soc.*, No. xxviii, January 1902.)

Mr. Carnegie, of the S.S. *Patrick Stewart*, reported that in 1906 in the entrance to the Persian Gulf the ship approached a patch which suddenly broke into life and brilliant light.

Bars of light travelled at 100 to 200 miles an hour about 20 feet apart and quite regular. This went on for a quarter of an hour, then all became dark for four minutes or so, and then they ran into a similar display which lasted some five or six minutes. The water was examined but nothing visible found in it. (*See Journal of the R. Meteorological Soc.*, No. xxxii, October 1906.)

Allowing for difference of observers these two accounts are similar in the general character of the display, and show that some impulse, acting in intermittent waves, affects the light-giving organisms. Here is another description, by Mr. S. C. Patterson, of S.S. *Delta*, in the northern entrance to the Straits of Malacca in March 1907 at 2 A.M. He saw shafts of pale yellow light moving rapidly over the surface of the water, at first like spokes, 300 yards long, of a wheel, and then in waves one behind the other, that is, parallel. The rays travelled rapidly and the intervals between were very short. The phenomenon lasted about half an hour over a distance of six miles. It ceased suddenly. The sea was smooth, sky cloudy, air temperature 83°, and there were no brilliant patches of phosphorescence about. The interesting point about these displays is the impulse that seems to affect the bacteria almost instantaneously in waves.

Sir Sydney Olivier pointed out to the writer, when in Jamaica, a similar intermittent impulse occurring among the fire-flies. As far as the eye could see the light of a fire-fly there would be at one moment hundreds of these little lamps showing, and the next would be all darkness. What adds to the weirdness of the display is the complete silence that accompanies them. H. de V. Stacpoole in the "Blue Lagoon" writes, "So many lamps ablaze that the firmament filled the mind with the idea of a vast and populous city—yet from all that living and flashing splendour not a sound."

But the fish themselves secrete a mucus which is also an illuminant. Some are furnished with a gland which, like those of the fire-fly, secretes a slowly oxidizing phosphorescent grease. A lateral line of small spots can be seen on most fish and this is a slime canal, from which, and from canals in the head and gill-covers, a mucus can be discharged at will, which no doubt facilitates passage through the water, besides being an illuminant. There are many special light-giving organs ranging from a simple pearly patch of skin up to a structure having a strong resemblance to a miniature bulls-eye lantern.

Some of the crustacea pour out from the base of the antennæ

FIG. 100. Commercial Sponges. *Euspongia officinalis zimmoca.*

copious clouds of a ghostly blue light sufficient to illuminate a bucket of sea water and make all its contents clearly visible.

It is thus evident that the ocean depths are here and there well lit up; but whether it is all illuminated, or whether deep-sea creatures have special sense organs enabling them to seek food or avoid danger with success, is not yet known.

The Prince of Monaco quotes the capture of an annelid, several inches in length, which was so transparent that its presence in a bowl of water could only be detected by the disturbance its progress created in a crowd of other animals.

A small angler-fish, *Melanocetus*, appears to live at the

lower limit of the sun's rays, below 500 fathoms. It is black and it fishes with a luminous bait, and one or two instances are known of its swallowing other fish which do not go below that limit, and which therefore probably see imperfectly at that depth and are easily deceived with the decoy.

A. C.

CHAPTER X

OLD SEA MONSTERS

HAVING now touched lightly on life in the ocean as it exists at the present time, it may be of interest to describe life as it appeared to our early explorers.

Navigators of olden days, indeed, went to sea with their hearts in their mouths. Vivid representations of the leviathans of the deep were depicted on the ancient charts scouring the seas in the localities which they were supposed to dominate. In an atmosphere of superstition the unseen and the imperfectly seen are always terrible. Every voyager on his return gained repute by magnifying the risks he had run from dimly perceived uncouth monsters in the ocean.

The Narwhal became the Sea Unicorn; the Alligator, swept seaward out of a river, became the Sea Dragon; the Sunfish became the Teufelwal; the Octopus became the Hydra or the Kraken.

When we consider that only one hundred years ago a giant whirlpool capable of engulfing large vessels was believed to exist in the North Sea; that the probability of a warm open sea at the poles for six months in the year was seriously discussed; that the expression "Nature abhors a vacuum" was commonly taught in our schools; that the sun's varied illumination of the moon was deemed to directly affect our weather, it will be seen how imagination took the place of facts, through want of critical inquiry.

Charts were not only ornamented with imaginary sea monsters and whirlpools, but also with volcanic flames which burst up through the sea at certain points.

The mariner therefore put to sea prepared to meet with extraordinary phenomena and to be attacked by fearsome beasts; and he took with him an imagination sufficient to endow the most inoffensive turtle with destructive powers.

FIG. 101. Sea Monsters.

The *Nahual* (Narwhal). If any man eat of this fish, he dieth presently. It hath a tooth in the fore part of his head, standing out seven cubits [12 feet]. This divers have sold for the Unicorns horn. This monster is forty elles [120 feet] in length.

The *Roider*, a fish of a hundred and thirty elles [390 feet] in length, which hath no teeth. The flesh of it is very good meat, wholesome and toothsome.

The *Burchualur* hath its head bigger than all the body. It is threescore cubits [100 feet] long.

Hyena, the sea hogge, a monstrous kind of fish.

Ziphius, the sword-fish, an horrible sea monster, swallowing the black seal at one bitte.

The *English Whale*, thirty elles [90 feet] long: the tongue of it is seven elles [21 feet] in length.

Seenaut (Sea Cowes). They sometimes come out of the sea to feed upon the land. They have a little bagge hanging at their nose, by the help of which they live in the water: that being broken, they lie altogether upon the land, and do accompany themselves with other kine.

Rostunger. It goeth on the bottom of the sea upon foure feet, but very short ones. His skin may scarcely be pearced with any weapon. Hee sleepeth twelve hours together, hanging by his two long teeth upon some rocke.

That fear was the soil on which the seed of imagination sprouted is shown by the comparative absence of remarks in ancient works of that wonderfully real phenomenon the *flying-fish*. Size took first place, so that the whale and the sea lion, the basking shark and the octopus, originated the most awesome monsters.

Hearken to the description of a whale told by Claus Magnus, given in John Aston's interesting work, " Curious Creatures."

"There be many kinds of whales, some are hairy and of four acres in bigness, some are smooth skinned and those are smaller. Some have their jaws long and full of teeth, the latter 6, 8, or 12 foot long, but their two dog teeth are longer than the rest and underneath. This kind of whale hath a fit mouth to eat, and his eyes are so large that fifteen men may sit in the room of each of them, and sometimes twenty or more. His horns are 6 or 7 foot long, and he hath 250 upon each eye as hard as horn that he can stir stiff or gentle either before or behind. These grow to defend his eyes in tempestuous weather.

The whale hath upon its skin a superficies like the gravel [probably adherent barnacles] that is by the seaside, so that when he raiseth his back above the waters, sailors take it to be an island and land on it and light fires and are surprised and drowned by the whale suddenly sinking.

Their forms are horrible, their heads square all set with prickles, and they have long horns round about like a tree rooted up by the roots. The apple of the eye is of one cubit and is red and fiery coloured which in the dark night appears to fishermen afar off under waters as a burning fire.

He will sometimes raise himself beyond the sail yards and cast such floods of waters above his head which he had sucked in, that with a cloud of them he will often sink the strongest ships. . . .

This is a remarkably exaggerated mix-up of the whale and the walrus, of the uprooted floating tree, and the phosphorescent jelly-fish.

Listen to the description by the same author, who was Archbishop of Upsala in 1555, of the sea serpent :

He states that all Norwegian fishermen are agreed :

" That there is a Sea Serpent 200 feet long and 20 feet thick that lives in caves and rocks on the coast near Bergen. He leaves his aquatic lair in clear summer nights and going ashore devours calves, lambs, and dogs. At other times he goes seaward and feeds on lobsters, octopuses, and crabs. He hath commonly hair hanging from his neck a cubit long, sharp scales, and is black, and he hath flaming shining eyes. He puts up his head on high like a pillar and catcheth away men and devours them." . . .

Many and wonderful are the reports of sea serpents, and much matter has been written about them. Snakes in the sea in the tropics are not uncommon. On the coast of China a yellow banded snake will often be seen at the surface during the N.E. Monsoon. It attains a length of 5 feet and its bite is

FIG. 102.   Water Snake.

highly poisonous. Off the mouths of rivers, such as the Amazon, during heavy floods amphibious snakes are sometimes carried out to sea in great numbers, and an anaconda 20 or 30 feet long might under such circumstances be met with. It must be remembered that the bottom of the ocean has been as yet merely tickled with the explorer's dredge, and that an active creature like a snake is not at all likely to be captured by such means. The earth's land surface has undergone immense changes in climate and flora, and the ancient land monsters that thrived in the Jurassic period have passed away, partly owing to change of conditions, and later from the attacks of ubiquitous man, who preyed in turn on these un-wieldy giants. But conditions in the deep sea have as far as we know but little altered, and just as some of the shallow-water fish have taken to a deep-sea life, so it is possible that the Ichthyosaurus or the Plesiosaurus may have changed its habitat from shallow to deep waters ; and, owing to their concealment below, a few examples may have survived to this day. If this is so it would account for their very rare appearance on the surface as so-called sea serpents, where they would only be driven by some accident or sickness.

That one is easily misled by appearances every navigator knows. A line of discharged ashes with perhaps at the end of

FIG. 103. Sea Monsters. Figs. 101 and 103 drawn by Cadet E. S. Hynes, of the *Worcester*, from figures on an old chart (1585) kindly lent by E. Heawood, Esq., M.A.

The *Proshualur*, that is as much to say as the Sea Horse. It often doth the fisherman great hurt and skare. The greatest kind of *Whales*.

Skautuhvalur, somewhat like a ray or skaite. It is like an island, and with its finnes overturneth ships and boates.

Steipereidur, a most gentle and tame kind of whale: which for the defence of the fisherman fighteth against other whales. It is forbidden by proclamation that no man may kill or hurt this sort of whale. It is in length 100 cubits at the least.

Staukul. He hath been seen to stand a whole day together upright upon his taile. It is a very dangerous enemy to seamen and fishes, and greedily seeketh after mans flesh.

it an empty cask with straw sticking out of it, thrown overboard by the steward, forms, in smooth weather when there is a sleepy swell running, a most excellent sea serpent. The writer on his twenty-fifth year of sea service once called a boat away and jumped into it himself and pulled with all speed to rescue two poor fellows waving from an upturned boat after a typhoon in China seas. The object pulled to proved to be part of a tree with two white gulls seated on it sunning their wings! This was in broad daylight.

The whale not uncommonly rises two thirds of its length out of water and falls heavily back, making a terrible splash. This is done to shake off parasites, and may alarm a small vessel near. The writer saw at Valparaiso, in 1875, the crew of a schooner take to their boat and temporarily desert their ship, which lay at anchor in the line of a whale performing this antic.

If deep-sea Saurians still exist it is, however, curious that the dead body of one has not been found floating on the surface or washed ashore. Whales, basking sharks, and large cuttle-fish are not uncommonly stranded, but these monsters may be reckoned in millions compared to a possibly few surviving Saurians.

The cuttle-fish, either Calamary or Octopus, is no doubt responsible for the legend of the many-headed Hydra, and it is indeed a terrible beast with which to contend. It seldom attacks boats, and is then probably ignorant that men are directing the craft. Well authenticated specimens have been secured, either by their having been washed ashore after death, or caught in nets, or by their limbs having been chopped off by those they attacked. An entire specimen was preserved at St. John's, Newfoundland, whose body was 8 feet long while its longest arms were 24 feet. It had about eighty suckers on each of the long arms. This specimen, however, was not a full-grown one, and they may attain still greater dimensions.

H.M. surveying vessels were employed for many years in proving the non-existence of dangerous reefs in the open ocean. Cruising in the then unknown waters of the Hainan Gulf in China, the writer once ordered all the young seamen of his ship to go aloft, and, pointing out a yellow sand-bank on which the calm sea seemed to be lazily lapping, he called the attention of the look-out man to the fact that he ought to have seen the danger from aloft before it was seen from deck. The ship was then hove to and a boat was sent to examine the shoal. To the surprise of all on board the boat returned and reported that the yellow patch was simply a field of minute marine algæ, termed by sailors whale's spawn !

It has been shown in these pages that there is much of interest on the sea surface for any observer with good sight, that there is a great deal more for those who have the leisure and appliances for probing the depths; but care must be taken not to let the imagination run riot, and whenever possible the discoverer should prove, by producing the whole or at least a portion of the prize, that his discovery is no chimera.

A. C.

CHAPTER XI

WEATHER

SEVENTY per cent. of the globe surface is under ocean. Geographically this vast extent of water is distributed as follows (Chart facing page 6) : the Atlantic Ocean, the Pacific Ocean, the Indian Ocean, and the Arctic and Antarctic Oceans. Included in the ocean areas are their several seas, gulfs, bays, etc. In the Atlantic, for instance, are the Gulf of Mexico, the Caribbean Sea, the North Sea, the Irish Sea, the Channel, the Bay of Biscay, and the Mediterranean Sea. In the Pacific Ocean are the Seas of China and Japan, and the Sea of Okhotsk. In the Indian Ocean are the Bay of Bengal, the Seas of the East Indian Archipelago, the Red Sea, Persian Gulf, etc. The Arctic Ocean includes the Greenland Seas, Behring Sea, and all the waters of the Arctic Circle above 60° N. Lat. The Antarctic Ocean includes all the South Polar waters from 60° S. Lat. The Atlantic, Pacific, and Indian Oceans are the great highways of shipping : on them the naval and mercantile vessels of the world unceasingly come and go.

The meteorological conditions over those vast ocean areas are still somewhat conjectural, although the key to the most baffling weather phenomena must be sought in these wide unimpeded air spaces.

Weather is an important matter to ocean travellers, whose comfort—if not safety—is dependent on it. To some extent certain conditions may be expected in certain localities; for instance, a fairly equable temperature is the rule on the Atlantic voyage to America. All varieties of temperature are experienced in the course of a voyage from England to

Australia. It may begin in chilly, damp, foggy, or boisterous weather lasting perhaps till entering the (usually) delightful run in the Mediterranean, which is followed by the hot dry temperature of the Suez Canal and Red Sea passages. The

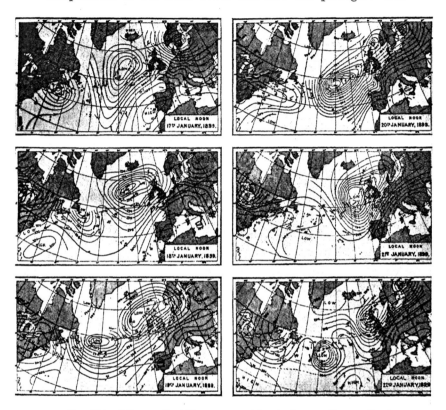

FIG. 104. "Passage" of Storm across Atlantic Ocean. From a Chart issued by the Meteorological Office.

moist warmth of the Indian Ocean is succeeded by the pleasant temperature prevailing off the Australian coasts.

Weather of whatever sort may be attributed to the difference of temperature at the poles and at the equator. The action and reaction of heat on cold and of cold on heat produces a weather system which doubtless operates, fundamentally, in a uniform way, but which, owing to the irregular distribution of land and sea and their opposing influences, is constantly subject to irregu-

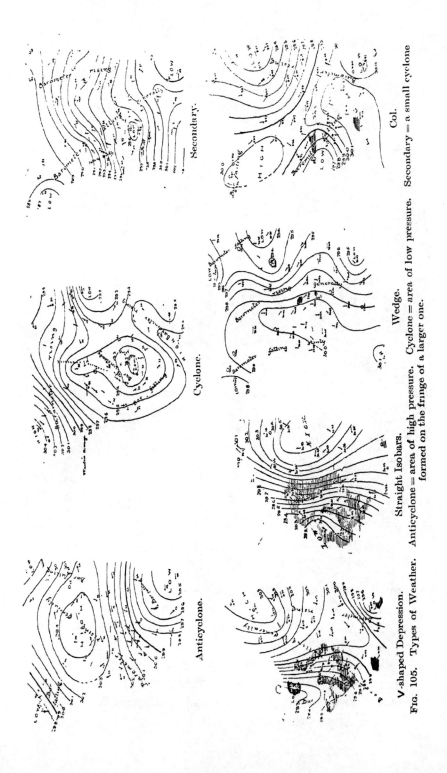

Secondary.

Cyclone.

Anticyclone.

Col.

Wedge.

Straight Isobars.

V-shaped Depression.

Fig. 105. Types of Weather.

Anticyclone = area of high pressure. Cyclone = area of low pressure. Secondary = a small cyclone formed on the fringe of a larger one.

larity and change. The difference in the speed of rotation of the earth on different parallels of latitude has a very important bearing on the direction of any moving object. For instance, a northerly wind becomes a north-easterly wind owing to this fact. Round the equator a hot, moist, vapour-laden atmosphere of moderate barometric pressure is constantly prevalent in a broad but somewhat irregular belt.

We have not yet sufficient data as to the true atmospheric conditions at the poles, but there apparently are wide areas of low barometric pressure subject to changes of temperature and to violent storms. On the equatorial side of the polar regions the " Brave West Winds " are met alternating with storms. Between this region and the equatorial belt is an area in which the wind blows fairly steadily from one quarter —a polar east direction—throughout the year. This is the region of the trade winds, an area of pleasant temperature and great evaporation. On the northern waters of the Indian Ocean the weather conditions are subjected to the disturbing influences of the Asiatic Continent, and here the " Trade Winds " are diverted and the monsoons replace them seasonally. These winds are really local " Trade Winds." In the Indian Seas the N.E. Trade blows in winter but not in summer, when, owing to the intense heat and the generation of indraft, the S.E. Trade Wind is drawn up far north, as a S.W. Monsoon Wind.

Monsoons occur in other localities, as in the East Indian Archipelago, the China Seas, on the West Coast of Africa, and on the West Coast of Central America.

The so-termed "permanent" belts of atmosphere are invaded and influenced by winds, calms, and moisture. This is the case especially in the calm belt about the equator, where torrential rains occur frequently, often accompanied by thunder, lightning, and waterspouts.

The general disposition of the barometric pressure is intimately connected with the direction of the wind. The Atlantic, Pacific, and Indian Ocean areas are formed of a more or less

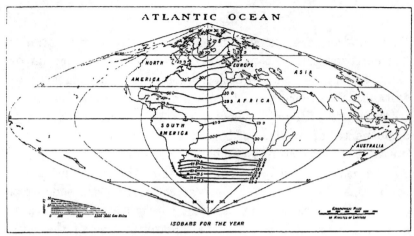

ATLANTIC OCEAN

ISOBARS FOR THE YEAR

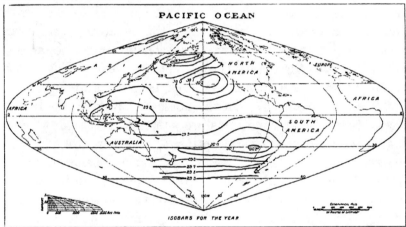

PACIFIC OCEAN

ISOBARS FOR THE YEAR

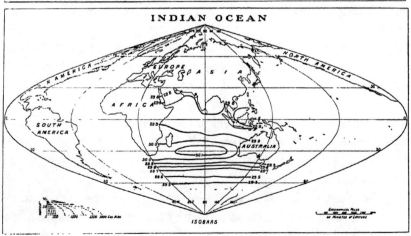

INDIAN OCEAN

ISOBARS

Fig. 106.

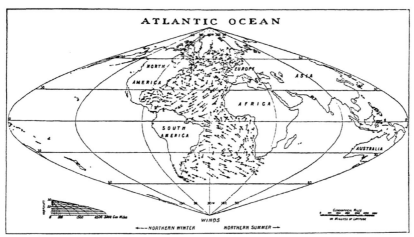

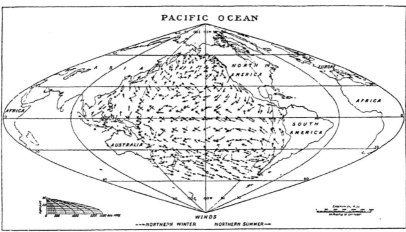

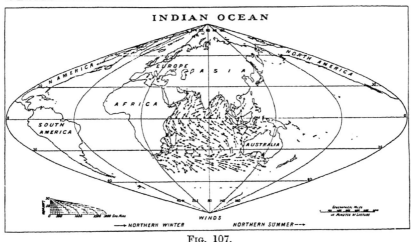

Fig. 107.

permanent high pressure. These areas surge or alter in position to and fro. Owing to the contracting area of the globe as the poles are approached, the parallel of 30° Lat. divides the hemispheres into equal parts, consequently the poleward travelling air on reaching a certain point must return again to the equator.

Certain investigations show that at a height in the atmosphere of about 7 miles a position of more or less stability of temperature is reached : this is called the isothermal layer. Weather conditions on the surface of the globe seem to be a good deal affected by the movements in and about this layer of atmosphere.*

In the high barometric areas, the surface currents of the ocean seem to circulate in unison with the wind currents. An inspection of the map will show how close is the connexion of winds with waters, though the waters are less liable to sudden change, and water currents are not deflected from their course nor increased in speed as quickly as are air currents. The sea currents in the Atlantic are the most remarkable and the most influential in their action on the atmosphere. The great Gulf Stream is the main factor in the beneficent climate of the western coasts of Europe. In the equatorial regions the ocean flow is westward (some counter currents are, however, met with here). On the eastern side of the western continents the ocean flow is polewards, some currents making away right into the polar seas, though the general flow turns east at a more southern point, so becoming westerly currents till, on striking the eastern continents, they are deflected towards the equator, completing a great ocean whirl, which has its counterpart in the whirl of the winds of the globe. The currents in the Pacific Ocean follow a similar plan of circulation, but in the Indian Ocean the circulation of currents is entirely altered by the land masses of Asia thrown out— as it were—far into the ocean on its north side. The plates

* It is quite possible for this layer to play an important part in the migration of birds (p. 65).

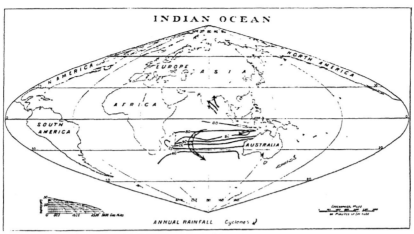

INDIAN OCEAN

ANNUAL RAINFALL   Cyclones

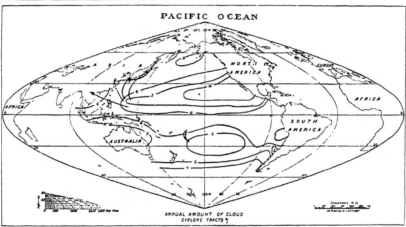

PACIFIC OCEAN

ANNUAL AMOUNT OF CLOUD
CYCLONE TRACTS

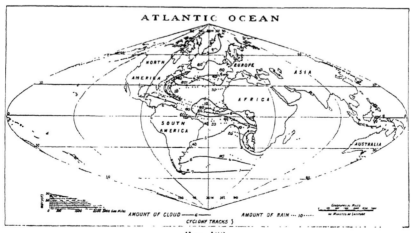

ATLANTIC OCEAN

AMOUNT OF CLOUD ——   AMOUNT OF RAIN ···10···
CYCLONE TRACKS

Fig. 108.

show the general trend and effects of the ocean currents; their ameliorating influence on the West European, West African and South American coasts, and the very chilling influence of the polar currents off the coast of Newfoundland in the northern hemisphere, and off the Falkland Islands in the southern hemisphere. These polar currents are the cause of heavy fogs, but are very helpful to life in the waters in which they flow.

In different latitudes the temperature of the air and water

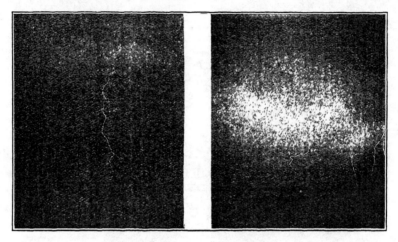

FIG. 109. Fork Lightning.

corresponds closely. The charts show how the ocean currents affect the air. In the polar regions the air currents—more especially the vertical currents—must be powerfully influenced by the ice. In the Atlantic the ocean flow is largely determined by the formation of the South American continent. The projection of the land at Cape St. Roque, to the south of the equator, forces northwards the main stream of the warm equatorial current, which swirls across the Atlantic as the Gulf Stream.

Some areas are subject at certain seasons to violent storms, differently designated according to locality. In the West Indies they are know as hurricanes, in the China Seas as typhoons, in India as cyclones. All are alike in extreme violence of intensity and great electrical displays. The following table gives the seasons at which these storms occur:

Table of Hurricane Seasons

West Indies
July
August ⎫
September ⎬ Max.
October ⎭
November

South Pacific
January
February
March
     (very few)

Bay of Bengal
May
June
October ⎫
November ⎭ Max.

Arabian Sea
April ⎫
May ⎪
June ⎬ Few
November ⎭

South Indian Ocean
November
December
January ⎫
February ⎬ Max.
March ⎭
April

China Seas
May
June
July
August
September, Max.
October
November

A storm of smaller extent, but often violent and usually accompanied by torrential rain and electrical disturbances in the atmosphere, is known as a tornado; it frequently occurs off the West Coast of Africa and in other localities.

The beauty of sunrise and sunset and the wonderful formations of clouds are nowhere better observed than at sea, where the view is from horizon to horizon. All clouds may be said to belong to one of two main types: to *Cumulus* or heap type, to *Stratus* or layer type. In the Cumulus type the cloud is thick and lumpish. In the Stratus it is layer-like, and sometimes more or less transparent to the sun and moon. At other times the layer of clouds is quite thick, as in the *Nimbus* or rain cloud.

It is noteworthy that one type of cloud prevails more than the other in certain ocean areas. In the north-east trade region great masses of stratus are met with, while in the south-east trade district the cumuliform clouds predominate. In the doldrums and the horse latitudes the cumulus type prevails, often in the most curious and remarkable forms. In the north-east trades a very high variety of stratus, known as cirrus (very thin, high, wispy or feathery-like clouds) is con-

Fɪɢ. 110.   Pillar Cumulus.

stantly to be seen working away to the north-east from a south-westerly direction. On the polar sides of the trades we find all varieties of clouds. Cirrus clouds are valuable indications of coming weather and of the distribution of atmospheric pressure in cyclonic disturbances. The few accompanying pictures with short description of clouds illustrate the different types.

The *Cumulus* type of clouds comprises five well-defined varieties as follows :

1. Fine-weather cumulus (Fig. 113, ɪ).

2. Shower cumulus, when rain falls without increase of wind ; the edges of the cloud are ragged but not cirrus-topped.

3. Squall cumulus, when rain, snow or hail falls, accompanied by a decided increase in the force of the wind (Fig. 113, H).

4. Pillar cumulus, noticeable in calm belts of ocean, is distinguishable by slender formations towering often to great altitudes. (Fig. 110).

5. Roll cumulus, characteristic of stormy winds, particularly of polar west winds which succeed cyclonic disturbances.

FIG. 111. Stratus (Fog Variety).

The *Stratus* type may be divided into four varieties :

1. Fog, really a dense cloud resting on the earth's surface (Fig. 111). It has been described as a cloud viewed from within.

2. Stratus, a dull-looking, sheet-like cloud which covers the sky at a moderate elevation and over large areas in anti-cyclonic conditions. Parallel lines appear in its under surface round the horizon. Here and there lighter patches are seen in the sky.

3. High stratus (cirro-cumulus), which includes all the mackerel skies, is a cloud which varies much in height. Sometimes it floats at but a moderate elevation ; at other times

Fig. 112. High Stratus (Cirro-cumulus)

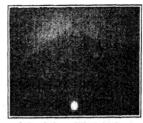

A. Cirrus radiant point; first warning of approaching storm.

B. Cirrus threads parallel to horizon and 90° from radiant point.

c. Solar halo. Wind freshening and barometer falling.

D. Dense cirro-stratus, slowly turning to nimbus. Spots of rain.

E. Nimbus. Rain falling; wind freshening to gale; barometer falling fast.

F. Centre of storm. Nimbus cloud lifting on polar west horizon. Barometer inclined to rise, and wind shifting to polar quadrant.

G. Barometer rising. Dense cloud passing off with cirri from edge. Wind blowing freshly from polar west.

H. Squall cumulus clouds in rear of storm. Barometer rising.

I. Fine weather. Barometer steady. Cumulus.

FIG. 113. Clouds illustrating Passage of Storm directly over an observer in High Latitudes.

it is seen floating in beautiful nubecules high up in the atmo-
sphere. The nubecules are caused by cross currents of air.
This is a cloud of warning which should be carefully watched
(Fig. 112).

4. Cirrus, often called mare's tails, the highest form of cloud
known, is composed of ice crystals. It floats at a great elevation in the atmosphere. It is of little importance when it is
present only as scattered fragments or wisps of cloud, but when
it appears in parallel lines or sheets on the horizon or as if

D. W.-B.

FIG. 114. Cloud Shadows.

radiating up in streamers from a particular point of the horizon,
it is distinctly a cloud of warning and should be carefully
watched in connexion with the movements of the barometer.
The various halos, mock-suns, parhelia, etc., are caused by
the shining of the sun through this cloud, in the various conditions in which it appears. (Fig. 113, A, B, D, G).

A variety of cirrus seems to edge the squall cumulus cloud
and is a good warning of approach (Fig. 113, H).

Nimbus, the cloud from which rain falls steadily and continuously, seems to be a gradual thickening downward of the
cirrus cloud (Fig. 113, E, F).

Both types of cloud are often found intermingled; this

shows a disturbed state of the atmosphere, as does "scud," a name given to the thin fine fragments of cloud sometimes seen hurrying across the sky with great rapidity.

Cloud shadows, which are rays due to shadows cast by the sun shining through stratus clouds, are fairly common as beautiful effects at sea. Their appearance has given rise to different legends. In England the phenomenon is called the "Sun drawing up water." In the Sandwich Islands the rays are known as "The Ropes of Maui." The following legend is from the "Myths and Songs of the South Pacific," by W. W. Gill.

The Legend of Maui

Maui was the great hero of the Pacific and had already not only discovered the secret of fire for the use of mortals, but had elevated the sky above the earth. The sun, however, had a trick of setting every now and then, so that it was impossible to get through any work; even an oven of food could not be prepared and cooked before the sun had set, nor could an incantation to the gods be chanted through ere the world was overtaken by darkness. Now Ra, or the Sun, is a living creature and divine, in form resembling a man, and possessed of fearful energy; his golden locks are displayed morning and evening to mankind. But Tatanga advised her son not to have anything to do with Ra, as many had at different times endeavoured to regulate his movements, and had signally failed; but the redoubtable Maui was not to be discouraged, and resolved to capture the sun-god Ra. Maui now plaited six great ropes of strong cocoa-nut fibre, each of four strands, and of a great length. He started off with his ropes to the distant aperture through which the sun climbs up from Avaiki, or the land of ghosts, into the heavens and there laid a slip noose for him. Farther on in the sun's path a second trap was laid—in fact all the six ropes were placed at distant intervals along the accustomed route of Ra. Very early in the morning the unsuspecting sun clambered up from Avaiki to perform his usual journey through the heavens. Maui was lying in wait near the first noose, and exultingly pulled it; but it slipped down the sun's body and only caught his feet. Maui ran forward to look after the second noose, but that likewise slipped

K

through, luckily it closed round the sun's knees. The third caught him round the hips, the fourth round the waist, the fifth under the arms; still the sun went tearing on his path, scarcely heeding the contrivances of Maui; but happily for Maui's designs the sixth and last of nooses caught the sun round the neck. Ra, or the Sun, now terribly frightened, struggled hard for his liberty; but to no purpose, for Maui pulled the rope so tight

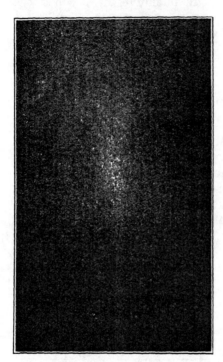

Fig. 115.   Sun Pillar.

as almost to strangle the sun, and then fastened the end of his rope to a point of rock. Ra, now nearly dead, confessed himself to be vanquished; and fearing for his life, gladly agreed to the demand of Maui that he should be in future a little more reasonable and deliberate in his movement through the heavens, so as to enable the inhabitants of this world to get through their employments with ease. The sun-god Ra was now allowed to proceed on his way; but Maui wisely declined to take off these ropes, wishing to keep Ra in constant fear.

These ropes may still be seen hanging from the sun at dawn, and when he descends into the ocean at night. By the assistance of the ropes he is gently let down into Avaiki, and in the morning raised up out of the shades; while the islanders still say when they see rays of light diverging from the sun, "Tena te Taura a Maui" (" Behold the ropes of Maui ").

In Ceylon the clouds are called " Buddha's Rays," and in Denmark "Locke is drawing water."

Less beautiful rays or shadows are cast upwards at times from the edges of the cumulus clouds. Sometimes beautiful

prismatic colours occur in high stratus clouds of the cirro-
cumulus variety when near the sun. Other striking phenomena, seldom noticed on land, are the rings round the sun
and moon, known as Halos or Coronæ. The halos appear at
some distance from the orb, the coronæ close to. A pillar of
light sometimes seems to rise from the setting sun : this
phenomenon is called a Sun Pillar. The " Green Flash " may
be seen sometimes just before the sun rises from, or sets below,

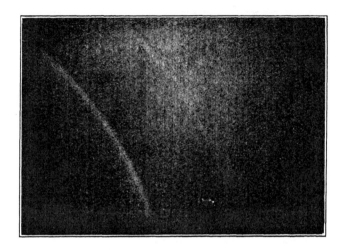

FIG. 116. A Double Rainbow.

the horizon, in a clear sky. Sometimes, before sunrise or just
after sunset, pink rays shoot up from where the sun is hidden
and stretch across the sky. There are also rainbows and " Sun
dogs." All such phenomena attract more attention at sea
than on land, and they add beauty and interest to the voyager's
way. Lightning effects and other electrical displays, such as
the *Aurora Borealis* and St. Elmo's Fire, may occur. St. Elmo's
Fire appears sometimes in stormy weather as a pale light at a
masthead or at the yardarms.

Fogs are perhaps the greatest danger to navigation. They
come as clouds resting on the sea, and are due to unusual ex-
tremes of different temperatures in the atmosphere and the

sea surface. In fogs, vessels have to rely for guidance chiefly on fog signals, a worrying necessity as sound miscarries considerably in fog. Thick mists are prevalent in the Red Sea and off the West Coast of Africa, owing to the presence of fine dust in the atmosphere. In the Mediterranean also the air may be charged with dust—fine grains of sand mixed with vegetable substances—which is borne on air currents probably

Fig. 117. Aurora Australis. 2 A.M., Dec. 9, 1881. Lat. 50° 52′ S. ;
Long. 160° 40′ W.

from the deserts to great distances on land and over sea. In the same way it occasionally happens that swarms of insects— butterflies, moths, dragonflies, and sometimes birds—are caught in a current of air and carried far out to sea, where they may settle on the rigging and deck of a ship coming in their track, causing delight—or annoyance—to those on board.

The weather bureaux of this country and of the United States have decided to adopt a new scientific nomenclature for the reading of the barometer and thermometer. By the courtesy of the Director of the Meteorological Office and for purposes of comparison, a table showing these differences is attached.   D. W.-B.

PRESSURE VALUES

*Equivalents in Millibars of Inches of Mercury at 32°
and Latitude 45°*

Mercury Inches	·00	·01	·02	·03	·04	·05	·06	·07	·08	·09
					MILLIBARS.					
27·0	914·3	914·6	915·0	915·3	915·7	916·0	916·3	916·7	917·0	917·4
27·1	917·7	918·0	918·4	918·7	919·0	919·4	919·7	920·1	920·4	920·7
27·2	921·1	921·4	921·8	922·1	922·4	922·8	923·1	923·4	923·8	924·1
27·3	924·5	924·8	925·1	925·5	925·8	926·1	926·5	926·8	927·2	927·5
27·4	927·9	928·2	928·5	928·9	929·2	929·5	929·9	930·2	930·6	930·9
27·5	931·2	931·6	931·9	932·3	932·6	932·9	933·3	933·6	933·9	934·3
27·6	934·6	935·0	935·3	935·6	936·0	936·3	936·7	937·0	937·3	937·7
27·7	938·0	938·3	938·7	939·0	939·4	939·7	940·0	940·4	940·7	941·1
27·8	941·4	941·7	942·1	942·4	942·8	943·1	943·4	943·8	944·1	944·4
27·9	944·8	945·1	945·5	945·8	946·1	946·5	946·8	947·2	947·5	947·8
28·0	948·2	948·5	948·8	949·2	949·5	949·9	950·2	950·5	950·9	951·2
28·1	951·6	951·9	952·2	952·6	952·9	953·2	953·6	953·9	954·3	954·6
28·2	954·9	955·3	955·6	956·0	956·3	956·6	957·0	957·3	957·7	958·0
28·3	958·3	958·7	959·0	959·3	959·7	960·0	960·4	960·7	961·0	961·4
28·4	961·7	962·1	962·4	962·7	963·1	963·4	963·7	964·1	964·4	964·8
28·5	965·1	965·4	965·8	966·1	966·5	966·8	967·1	967·5	967·8	968·1
28·6	968·5	968·8	969·2	969·5	969·8	970·2	970·5	970·9	971·2	971·5
28·7	971·9	972·2	972·6	972·9	973·2	973·6	973·9	974·2	974·6	974·9
28·8	975·3	975·6	975·9	976·3	976·6	977·0	977·3	977·6	978·0	978·3
28·9	978·6	979·0	979·3	979·7	980·0	980·3	980·7	981·0	981·4	981·7
29·0	982·0	982·4	982·7	983·0	983·4	983·7	984·1	984·4	984·7	985·1
29·1	985·4	985·8	986·1	986·4	986·8	987·1	987·5	987·8	988·1	988·5
29·2	988·8	989·1	989·5	989·8	990·2	990·5	990·8	991·2	991·5	991·9
29·3	992·2	992·5	992·9	993·2	993·5	993·9	994·2	994·6	994·9	995·2
29·4	995·6	995·9	996·3	996·6	996·9	997·3	997·6	997·9	998·3	998·6
29·5	999·0	999·3	999·6	1000·0	1000·3	1000·7	1001·0	1001·3	1001·7	1002·0
29·6	1002·4	1002·7	1003·0	1003·4	1003·7	1004·0	1004·4	1004·7	1005·1	1005·4
29·7	1005·7	1006·1	1006·4	1006·8	1007·1	1007·4	1007·8	1008·1	1008·4	1008·8
29·8	1009·1	1009·5	1009·8	1010·1	1010·5	1010·8	1011·2	1011·5	1011·8	1012·2
29·9	1012·5	1012·8	1013·2	1013·5	1013·9	1014·2	1014·5	1014·9	1015·2	1015·6
30·0	1015·9	1016·2	1016·6	1016·9	1017·3	1017·6	1017·9	1018·3	1018·6	1018·9
30·1	1019·3	1019·6	1020·0	1020·3	1020·6	1021·0	1021·3	1021·7	1022·0	1022·3
30·2	1022·7	1023·0	1023·3	1023·7	1024·0	1024·4	1024·7	1025·0	1025·4	1025·7
30·3	1026·1	1026·4	1026·7	1027·1	1027·4	1027·7	1028·1	1028·4	1028·8	1029·1
30·4	1029·4	1029·8	1030·1	1030·5	1030·8	1031·1	1031·5	1031·8	1032·2	1032·5
30·5	1032·8	1033·2	1033·5	1033·8	1034·2	1034·5	1034·9	1035·2	1035·5	1035·9
30·6	1036·2	1036·6	1036·9	1037·2	1037·6	1037·9	1038·2	1038·6	1038·9	1039·3
30·7	1039·6	1039·9	1040·3	1040·6	1041·0	1041·3	1041·6	1042·0	1042·3	1042·6
30·8	1043·0	1043·3	1043·7	1044·0	1044·3	1044·7	1045·0	1045·4	1045·7	1046·0
30·9	1046·4	1046·7	1047·1	1047·4	1047·7	1048·1	1048·4	1048·7	1049·1	1049·4

CHAPTER XII

WAVES

THE modern steamer towers above the waves and, as a rule, is invulnerable to their onslaught. But only the other day the disastrous possibilities of a great wave were demonstrated when a large new steamer was struck by one in the Pacific and immediately broke in two, the after part sinking at once, while the fore part, being lighter and protected by bulkheads, floated for a time. The destructive power of waves often makes havoc along the coasts in a heavy gale.

The ever-varying movements of the sea's surface are due to the striking of the wind on the water and the consequent formation of waves. There are many sorts of waves : waves of air, of light, of sound, of electricity, etc., in all of which the underlying principle is the propagation of movement without transmission of material. A familiar illustration of this fact is found by throwing a stone into a pool, when a series of concentric (Fig. 118) waves will immediately pass out from the spot where the stone sank. Sea waves are not, however, due to such a cause, but are the result of the ruffling of the surface by the striking of the wind. As the wind increases the waves rise higher and higher, until, in wide oceanic areas, we get the great waves which strike the beholder with admiration and wonder. As the amount of friction between air and water can be but slight, it is surprising that waves are so quickly raised by the wind. The probable explanation is that once the first ripples are started, the wind gains increase of power by the

150

increased surface offered to it.* And as the wind grows in violence the waves grow in size, to a certain point. In the open oceans, the waves, as a rule, run with the wind ; that is to say, the wave crests and their troughs are at right angles to the direction of the wind ; but the trend of the sea does not immediately respond to a change in the direction of the wind, and we get what are known as cross seas before the waves alter their course. When the wind drops suddenly, the sea

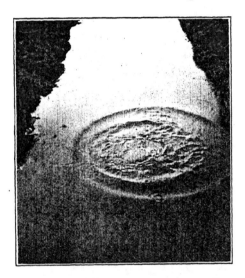

FIG. 118. Circular Waves produced by throwing a Stone into Water.

does not at once relapse into calm, but the " heads " or " tops " of the waves become topheavy and curl over to a much greater degree than when the wind was blowing : this phase, however, soon passes, and a heavy swell, sometimes lasting a considerable time, supervenes. On the other hand, should the wind suddenly increase in force, as in a squall, the wave tops are torn off and scattered about in the fine spray form known as " *spoon-drift*," which often fills the air to some height and looks like a white mist. Innumerable wavelets occur on the waves, and the sea takes on the appearance of a seething cauldron. In such

* The wind also in passing over the surface appears to cause a drawing-up action in the wave crests with a depressing action in the troughs.

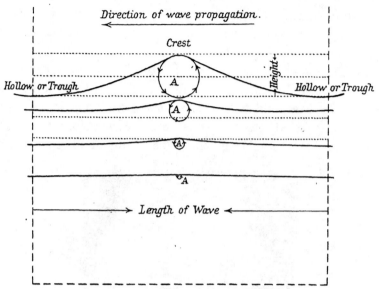

FIG. 119.   Section of a Trochoidal Wave illustrating parts of wave and movements of water particles A.

Photo by Capt. Corner

FIG. 120.   A Fine Roller in High South Latitudes.

violent squalls the wind is often said to beat down the sea. After such an experience, the rigging to the tops of the masts is frequently found covered with fine particles of salt.   Waves appear to race along at a great speed, but this is more an apparent than actual fact. The same sort of motion may be seen on a cornfield blown upon by the wind : the change of colour, due to the bending of the cornstalk heads, makes these appear to be actually moving forward. What occurs in sea waves is that the particles of water in the upper part (Fig. 119) of the wave do move or swing forward to a certain

Photo by J. Elmslie

FIG. 121.   Rough Sea off Cape Horn.

extent : this forward swing is counterbalanced by a backward movement or swing in the lower depths of the wave. The particles of water describe circles, of which the diameters are larger in the upper part of the wave, and diminish to nothing at its base.

Fig. 127 illustrates a *following* sea. When a ship is running before the wind and sea there is a danger of her being pooped. This happens when, through the dropping of the wind for a moment or two, the *periods* of the ship and the wave alter, with the result that the stern does not rise soon enough and the sea comes on board.

A sailor soon knows instinctively when a sea is going to break aboard, and it is seldom that he is caught quite unawares. Fig. 131 shows a heavy sea coming aboard by the main rigging.

In the deep waters of the open oceans, the waves have a free run practically without friction; but directly they approach shallow water friction affects the bases of the waves, their heights diminish and they topple or curl over, as we can see

Photo by W. G. Klein

FIG. 122.   Strong North-West Gale in North Atlantic.

for ourselves any day on a beach. There is, it is true, a certain amount of " heave " in the sea, due to the throwing forward of what is floating on the surface; there is also the drawback or suction below, familiar to all bathers, which can be noticed also when a sea breaks on a pebbly beach.

Waves are measured by their *height*, which is the distance from trough to crest, and by their *length*, which is the distance from crest to crest or (Fig. 119) from trough to trough : their breadth is their extent along the crest.

The *period* of a wave is the time it takes to travel its own length. While there is no apparent connexion between wave height and length, there is a connexion between *wave speed*, *wave length*, and *wave frequency*. Figs. 120 to 128 show varying types of waves.

Curious streaks, marks and oily patches are often noticed on the sea. Doubtless, in many cases, these are due to the presence of myriads of minute organisms. Sometimes the oily patches are the trail left by a whale in its passage along the surface of the sea ; but not all surface markings are so to be explained. When a brisk wind is blowing, peculiar streaks appear and, if looked at through a powerful glass, a line of bubbles will be seen running down the centre of the streaks. Similar streaks occur when heavy rain drops are falling thickly on the sea. Such phenomena are worth investigation.

In comparing the heights of waves with the force of the wind, observers must be careful to make allowance for the fact that the sea rises more slowly and falls less rapidly than the wind. The height of waves is affected by the depth of the water ; they attain their greatest altitude in the southern oceans, where the great deep seas have a clear sweep round the world.*

HEIGHT OF WAVES IN FEET

	C. Desbois	Paris	Wilson-Barker
Hurricane . . .	28·54	25·43	28
Strong gale . .	20·67	16·57	23
Gale . . .	15·42	..	14
Strong breeze . .	10·83	..	8

In such shallow waters as the North Sea, waves are short and broken, though they are often a good height ; the sea, in

* Dr. Vaughan Cornish, in *Knowledge*, 1901, summarized the results of the observations of Paris, Desbois, and Wilson-Barker in comparisons of wave height with wind force as follows. These observers worked independently and without a knowledge of what the others were doing.

consequence, has an angrier appearance in rough weather than in the open oceans.

Waves have been reported up to 70 * feet in height, but

Photo by Capt. Wilson-Barker

FIG. 123. Calm with " cats'-paws."

Photo by Capt. Wilson-Barker

FIG. 124. Slight Air over Water, showing " oily " patches.

50 feet is more likely the accurate estimate of their extreme limit, which is rarely reached. In heavy gales in the high

* Such waves belong to the same class of phenomena as the 1000-feet icebergs.

southern latitudes they may reach a height of from 30 to 40
feet, and in the gales of the Atlantic and Pacific oceans 20 to 35
feet is not unusual.

Photo by Capt. Wilson-Barker

FIG. 125. Ripples.

Photo by Capt. Wilson-Barker

FIG. 126. Wavelets.

The easiest and commonest method of measuring wave
heights is to ascend the rigging or other elevation in the ship,*

* First recommended by Dr. Scoresby, an indefatigable observer of waves, and,
indeed, of all nautical phenomena.

and from that point to get the crest of the wave in line with the eye and the horizon : this will give, approximately, the height of the wave. Better results may be had by taking observations from amidships by means of a batten. A sensitive aneroid will show the change of level of the vessel as a wave passes beneath her. All such observations should be taken several times in succession to ensure a near approach to accuracy. Two observers should co-operate to take the period

Photo by Capt. Corner

FIG. 127.   Ship in High Sea, running before wind and sea.   Trough and crest are shown.

of a wave : while one observes the wave by fixing on a certain point and singing out " stop " as it passes a given spot in the rigging or other part of the ship, the second observer watches the time and duly notes it. In making these observations, the true course and speed of the ship, and the direction and force of the wind and of the sea, should all be noted. Waves often vary considerably in size. In a series A, B, C, D, E, F, G, H ; A and G may be quite big waves ; from A to D the size may diminish ; D to G it may increase. *Cross seas* at times break up the sea to such an extent that it is impossible to distinguish one set of waves from another. This occurs particularly when gales follow one another in rapid succession, forming fresh series of waves as they pass. In the high southern latitudes a succession of westerly gales constantly follow one on the other. In these gales the strongest wind is from the S.W., and an almost continual swell from that direction is the consequence. As a rule, however, the gale starts in the N.N.E. or N.,* and it is interesting to note the dark shadow, caused by the rising N.N.E'ly wind, crossing over the S.W'ly swell, until at last the S.W. sea is smoothed down by the N.N.E'ly gale, only to spring into force again directly the wind shifts to W. and S.W.

The passage of ships through the water is affected by (*a*) *skin-friction* between the hull of the vessel and the particles of water ; (*b*) *eddy-resistance* ; (*c*) *wave-resistance*. (*b*) and (*c*) are caused by the ship steaming at the surface of the sea ; (*b*) is also largely the result of friction. In the case of (*c*) we find that a vessel in her passage through the water forms four distinct systems of waves—the *oblique*

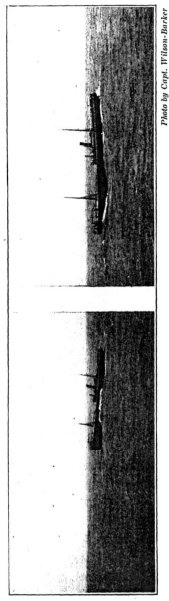

Photo by Capt. Wilson-Barker

Fig. 128. A Steamer diving into a Head Sea (θ). Trough and crest are shown.

* But the northerly sea never reaches anything like the height of the south-westerly sea.

bow and *stern waves*; the *transverse* and *rear waves*: of these, the bow waves are the most important. One can easily observe these waves for oneself. The late Mr. Froude, from such observations, founded the laws of "*corresponding speeds*" and "*resistance to motion due to wave-making*," by which builders are able to determine from models what the full-sized vessel will do. It has been demonstrated by ex-

Photo by Captain Wilson-Barker

FIG. 129.   Illustrating Method of noting Heel of Ships by means of photography, the angle in this case being 11° port.

periments that when a vessel is going at slow speed the resistance is mostly due to *skin-friction*; and that when going at high speed, the resistance is due to *wave-making*.

There is still much to learn as to the effect of waves on ships. A mathematician who would carefully study the problem in practical conditions at sea would have wide scope for the exercise of his science.

The action of the waves causes *rolling of ships* at sea. To minimise the consequent discomfort, bilge keels are now much in use, with the successful result that, in the large steamships, there is very little perceptible motion even in big seas. Observations on ship-rolling are most interesting, and they can be made simultaneously with wave observations. The roll of a ship from extreme port heel to extreme starboard heel is called a "swing"; if there is a reverse roll back to extreme port it is called a "*swing-swang*"; this roll should be timed in the same way as are wave *periods*. The angle of extreme heel may also be ascertained by using a clinometer, but it must be remembered that the ordinary clinometer registers a greater heel than is actually reached. Some clinometers of recent make give better results. They are constructed with mercury

FIG. 130. Wave Model (A) illustrating vessels (B) in waves following, B' on top of wave crest, sea on the beam, B" inside of wave, sea on the beam. Waves 250 feet long, vessel 500 feet long. By cutting out waves of different lengths and superimposing them in this set of waves, the effect of interference may be studied as well as the effect on vessels.

or spirits in a tube, the movement of the liquid being regulated by constriction of the tube. It is possible to get a photograph of the horizon which will accurately determine the angle of heel (Fig. 129). The camera should be placed on a level spot looking out directly over the bow (ahead) or over the stern (astern).

Fig. 130 gives some idea of the position of a vessel among waves. It is evident that the behaviour of a ship in a seaway, and the strains to which she is subjected, are governed to a great extent by the manner in which she is laden. This applies specially to modern vessels of great length, in which the longitudinal strains are considerable.

Pitching (Fig. 128) may be said to be rolling in a longitudinal direction. Although this motion is less disagreeable from the passenger's point of view, it is often a source of anxiety, as it causes much strain, particularly about the propellers of a steamer, and there may be a severe strain on the machinery

L

through the racing of the propeller caused by the shifting of the stern. Pitching, combined with the forward movement of the vessel, is in itself a cause of strain.

Before closing this chapter on Waves, I particularly wish to call the attention of sailors to a phenomenon of submarine waves which has lately been investigated by

Photo by W. Von Berg

FIG. 131. Running the Easting down. Shipping a heavy Sea.

oceanographers but of the existence of which most seamen are ignorant :

In such localities as the Norwegian fjords, in the Straits of Magellan, near the mouths of large rivers, wherever in fact river or glacier water meets the sea and flows out for any distance over the dense salt water below, a vessel may raise or create a large wave in the dense lower water strata which —though probably barely perceptible on the surface— will materially hinder and retard its progress. The ancients were familiar with this obstacle to navigation, and, unable to account for it, attributed it to the angry gods, who clutched, they said, the keel of the ship. Some believed that submarine monsters held back their vessel when they suffered this inconvenience. The matter is of importance, and has to be reckoned with when navigating the big deep ships of to-day in inshore waters.

D. W.-B.

CHAPTER XIII

SOME OLD SEA CUSTOMS AND CHANTEYS

WITH the rapidly disappearing sailing-ships of the past, we are losing sight of many old sea customs which formerly went far towards enlivening the tediousness of lengthy voyages.

Few may have the opportunity of witnessing some of the pastimes familiar to an older generation of travellers, so perhaps it will amuse and interest to hear details of some of them.

First, then, comes " The Dead Horse," though why known by that name is doubtful. It has been a general rule to advance to sailors, signing for a long voyage, a month's pay. This preliminary speaks for itself as to the thriftlessness of the profession ; sailors ashore seem bound to outstep their resources and to fall into debt, but probably in many cases the drawn wages are set aside as provision for a time for the family left at home. The curious point is that notwithstanding this overdrawn pay, seamen seem to have a rooted belief that the first month's work is unrewarded by any pay whatever ; they therefore look upon that month as a lost, wholly profitless period, and on its completion proceed to deal with it with special vengeance. For that purpose, the month is represented in effigy by a " dead " horse. That the custom grew and flourished was doubtless due to the fact that it served to amuse and divert successive generations of passengers, whose liberal purses were open to encourage any frolic of the sort.

The Horse—a very rough caricature of a noble animal—was manufactured of gunny bag and shavings ; two bottles did duty as eyes. The steed was mounted on a board supported by trucks taken for the occasion from the gun (all sailing-ships formerly carried a gun or guns). The second "dog watch" was the favourite hour for the performance, when the horse, ridden by a well-got-up jockey, was started from the fo'c'sle door; several grotesquely dressed figures pulled it along the deck, others accompanied the procession, while all the remainder of the crew brought up the rear.

FIG. 132. The Procession going Aft.

The horse was dragged aft to the poop, where the captain and passengers had assembled to await its coming. The cavalcade came along to the tune of a song, or chantey, which went as follows :

The Chantey Man sings : They say my horse is dead and
      gone.
Chorus : And they say so, and they hope so !
Chantey Man : They say my horse is dead and gone.
Chorus : Oh ! poor old man.
Chantey Man : For one long month I rode him hard.
Chorus : And they say so, and they hope so !

Chantey Man : For one long month I rode him hard.
Chorus : Oh ! poor old man.

And so on.

A halt was called at the quarter-deck, and a quaintly-dressed auctioneer proceeded briskly to put the animal up to the highest bidder.   This scene was the occasion of much chaff and laughter, and, when the hammer finally fell, it was to the tune of a good

FIG. 133. Neptune's Car.

round sum, afterwards to be divided among the crew.   A rope, led through a block on the lee main yardarm, was now attached to jockey and horse, and, to the accompaniment of a chantey—

Chantey Man : I'll hoist him to the main yardarm.
Chorus : And they say so, and they hope so !
Chantey Man : I'll hoist him to the main yardarm.
Chorus : Oh ! poor old man.

both were hoisted up to the yardarm ;   blue lights were burnt ; with three cheers the horse was cut adrift, and, immediately afterwards, a burning tar barrel was tossed overboard in his wake.

Another curious custom that was religiously observed at sea in the old days, was the initiation of all new-comers into his mysteries by Father Neptune himself. This ceremony took place when the novice crossed the line (or equator) for the first time. The proceedings opened the previous evening by the sudden appearance under the bows of a strange boat's crew.

FIG. 134. The Captain receives Neptune.

These men hailed the ship and were replied to from the poop by the captain, who demanded whence they came, and requested them to board his vessel. Four sailors, dressed in oilskins, obeyed his summons and came aft to the poop, where the captain shook hands with them and desired to be fully informed as to their business. They told him they were messengers from Father Neptune to all on board who, on the morrow, should cross the line for the first time ; that he bade them know he would personally attend their initiation into the secrets of his kingdom, and he warned all to await his coming at an appointed hour. The captain undertook the delivery of the messages or letters, gave each sailor a glass of grog, and they departed as they came.

The Letter

NEPTUNE'S COURT,
DEPTHS-OF-THE-SEA.

Father Neptune, by the Grace of Mythology, Lord of the Seas, Ruler of the Depths, and Sovereign of the Ocean, Hereby enjoins you

Name ....

to appear at His Court to be held on the upper deck of the good ship " . " at this day, to tender to Us homage, and to be initiated into the antient and mystic rites of His kingdom.

Given at His Court under the Equator,
the day of
(Signed)
NEPTUNE, R.

Next day, at 11 A.M., the arrival of Father Neptune and his retinue is announced. The Sea god appears, trident in hand, accompanied by Amphitrite, his wife, and a small boy, and they are followed by four or five policemen, a doctor, two barbers, a secretary, and four bears.

Some time previous to all this a sail had been stretched on one side of the deck, in sight of the poop ; this sail now holds a large amount of water. In front of the sail a platform is erected, on which the initiators and the luckless to-be-initiated are to stand. Neptune and Amphitrite are conducted in procession and are enthroned by the bulwarks, close to the water-filled sail, and, after being received by the captain, Neptune addresses him as follows :

Address of Neptune to the Captain

Gallant Captain of the good ship "   ," We welcome you and your ship's company to the centre of our domain. We understand that there are a number of novices here, and we have especial pleasure in welcoming them into our kingdom, and in initiating them into the mysteries of sea-dogs and enrolling them as our subjects.

Reply of Captain to Father Neptune

Most noble Father Neptune, Ruler of the Seas, and fair Amphitrite, on behalf of myself and my ship's company I thank you for the honour you have done us in coming on board, and for giving us such a hearty welcome to your domains.

Our novices have a sort of fearful joy in the approaching ceremony, and you can be sure of the honour they esteem it to become your subjects.

Meanwhile, Neptune's policemen search the ship for the new-comers, whose efforts at escape and concealment lead to wild chases and uproarious fun, but at last all submit to their fate, and are led in turn to a stool on the platform, where the barbers await each victim with huge wooden razors, often three feet long, with whitewash brushes and great buckets of lather made of flour and water. Close beside the barbers waits the doctor, provided with corks stuck with needles, wherewith to offer " salts " to the weaker neophytes. The captive being seated, the next move is to induce him to reply to some silly question ; no sooner does he open his mouth, than the watchful barber slops a brushful of lather into it, and his face and head are quickly smothered in the stuff, which is then scraped off with the wooden razors, and the victim is suddenly tipped backwards into the sail, to be caught and soundly ducked by the waiting bears. Sometimes the " doctor " sees fit to administer the restoring salts, when the struggles and protestations of the patient cause much fun; but he is not let off, it being clearly understood that he must go through with it to the bitter end. I must say that though I have been present on such occasions over and over again, I have never seen any unpleasantness or ill-feeling in consequence of this exceedingly uncomfortable practical joke; the initiated invariably bear the whole thing with great good-humour.

Fig. 135. A Victim under the Barber.

These ceremonies were generally followed by sports of various kinds, and a concert in the evening.

Dancing is a great amusement of sailors at sea, especially if there is a man among the crew who is a good violinist. It is certainly very funny to see two sailors dancing together, as they generally have a custom of placing the hands on one another's shoulders; yet the movements are graceful. It is said at sea that "Music hath charms to soothe the savage hog, the hungry midshipman, and the captain's dog," and it certainly requires very little inducement for the getting up of a "sing-song" when a number of sailors are gathered together.

The *Hornpipe* is very popular at sea, though only rarely is it danced in a merchant ship. It is much to be regretted that this dance is so little known.

While there is little that is original in the songs or chanteys of sailors, the method of singing them is distinctly novel and impossible to reproduce in set music. Only those who have heard them know the tune and style. It seems to be an instinct with men of all times and races to sing or " cry out," in

FIG. 136. A Victim in the Bath.

one fashion or another, when engaged at work requiring rhythm or regularity of movement. The old Egyptian crews carried a musician among their number, that his strains might help the rowers to pull in unison ; everywhere, throughout the world, men chant or sing for a like purpose. It is, too, a well-established fact that many animals, noticeably elephants, work better if accompanied by music or a song. Sailors' chanteys vary with the nature of their work. In ordinary pulling on a rope, one man " sings out."

To " heave oh-ing " a curious cry, which is generally far

from musical, I have never met but two men who " sang out " melodiously and sweetly ; their voices and their names have always remained in my memory—Svenson and Crunden. I do not know, but I presume the word " chantey ' is derived from the French verb *chanter*, to sing. The man who leads the others is called the " Chantey Man." When, on reaching port, sails are furled, particularly in the case of courses, which are heavy sails requiring concentrated effort to stow snugly

Fig. 137.   A Victim thrown into the Bath.

on top of the yard, the encouraging chorus was usually " Paddy Doyle's Boots," which went as follows :

> *Chantey Man :* With my aye, aye, aye, yah,
> *Chorus :* We'll pay Paddy Doyle for his boots.

The old wooden ships were constantly in need of pumping ; the well was frequently sounded, and this duty took place once generally in every watch. When the pumping was prolonged, a chantey was sung.

The Saucy Sailor Boy

1. He was a saucy sailor boy
    Who'd come from afar,
   To ask the maid to be the bride
    Of a poor Jack Tar.

2. The maiden, a poor fisher girl,
    Stood close by his side.
   With scornful look she answered thus :
    " I'll not be your bride."

And so on.

There were anchor songs to accompany the heaving up of an anchor, either by windlass or capstan. Such were :

Leave Her, Johnny

Solo : I thought I heard the skipper say
Chorus : Leave her, Johnnie, leave her !
Solo : To-morrow you will get your pay,
Chorus : It's time for us to leave her.
Solo : The work was hard, the voyage was long,
Chorus : Leave her, Johnnie, leave her !
Solo : The seas were high, the gales were strong,
Chorus : It's time for us to leave her.

A stirring one was :

Homeward Bound

Chantey : Our anchor we'll weigh, and our sails we will set.
Chorus : Good-bye, fare-ye-well ! Good-bye, fare-ye-well !

Chantey : The friends we are leaving we leave with regret !
Chorus : Hurrah ! my boys, we're homeward bound.

The first *sail-setting* chantey to which I had an introduction was " Haul the Bowline." It was on the occasion of my first voyage to sea, in February 1874. We were beating down the Channel against a strong S.W. gale. " All hands " was called, and we six new midshipmen somehow managed to get on deck with the rest. It was inky black, blowing hard and raining torrents. The sea outside was wild and angry, the ship pitched heavily, and on the deck dark forms clad in oilskins worked at a desperate fight with the elements. The chantey of the men engaged in setting the reefed upper main tops'il rose above the roar of the gale ; the curious, striking scene and the song fixed themselves in my memory, as did the personality of Crunden, a handsome swarthy sailor, who led the singing, and whom I afterwards knew to be as fine a seaman as I have ever met.

Haul the Bowline

Solo : Haul on the bowline, fore and main-top bowline.
Chorus : Haul on the bowline ! the bowline haul !
Solo : Haul on the bowline ! the packet is a-rolling
Chorus : Haul on the bowline ! the bowline haul !
Solo : Haul on the bowline ! the skipper he's a-growling :
Chorus : Haul on the bowline ! the bowline haul !

Opportunity was often taken in singing these chanteys to make obnoxious remarks regarding the " powers that be " in the rhyme, but no exception was taken to this.

Blow, Boys, Blow

Solo : A Yankee ship came down the river.
Chorus : Blows, boys, blow !

Solo : Her masts did bend, her sails did shiver.
Chorus : Blow, my bully boys, blow !

Solo : The sails were old, her sails were rotten.
Chorus : Blow, boys, blow !

Solo : His charts the skipper had forgotten.
Chorus : Blow, my bully boys, blow !

These examples will, it is thought, give some idea of the chanteys in use at sea.

Among old customs was that against whistling on board ship. I remember being severely admonished by an " old

salt " for inadvertently doing so, the idea being that it brought
on bad weather. The real reason against it was probably the
fact that all orders at sea are preceded by the sound of the
bosun's whistle, which is to attract attention to the order which
immediately follows. If other whistling were allowed it would
cause confusion.

Many other curious little customs occur to me, and sailors'
yarns innumerable, and many very amusing. I shall, however,
conclude with a short list of passengers' questions, to which the
captain is supposed to find replies.

> Have you ever been shipwrecked ?
> Are there any whales in this latitude ?
> What is the best cure for sea-sickness ?
> Why are they always painting the ship ?
> Do you remember my cousin who sailed with you in —— ?
> What is the nearest land ?
> When shall we take the pilot on board ?
> What's the barometer doing ?
> Why does the anchor take longer to come up than go down ?
> Does it always rain here ?
> What run have we made ?
>
> D. W.-B.

APPENDIX

TRAVELLERS who are photographers, as are most people to some extent nowadays, have exceptional opportunities at sea for the exercise of their art. The clear light is an immense advantage. Even in dull weather, good results are the rule even with rapid exposures.

Photographs of clouds, waterspouts, waves, and other phenomena are of much value in the study of meteorology. Pictures taken of birds in flight or at rest, of fishes and other animals swimming, jumping, etc., may all add to our knowledge of natural history. Good binoculars and a pocket lens, with a large flat field, equivalent to about one inch are useful aids in the examination of water life specimens.

Many naturalist photographers are doing much in England to increase our knowledge of wild creatures and to popularize the study of natural history. Beautiful pictures are to be found in Messrs. C. Griffin's " Open Air Series," in " Wild Life," and " Country Life," and elsewhere are the camera studies of such men as Kearton, Low, Ponting, Douglas English, Kirk, and others who specialize in Natural History subjects.

D. W.-B.

GLOSSARY

Actinozoa. Polypes or Zoophytes in which the mouth opens into a short tube which in turn opens into the general cavity of the body.

Amphipods. Small crustaceans having laterally compressed bodies.

Alcyonarians. Fleshy, Spongy, and Horny Corals.

Algæ. A general name for sea plants, mostly minute.

Ascidian. See Tunicates.

Bathymetrical. Measure, or contour, of depth.

Bathypelagic. Inhabiting the ocean depths.

Bryozoa. Minute composite animals forming plant-like colonies.

Calcareous. Composed of carbonate of lime.

Cephalopods. Cuttle-fishes and their allies.

Ciliæ. Movable microscopic hair-like filaments used for locomotion.

Copepods. Minute swimming crustaceans found in both fresh and salt water.

Crinoids. Lily-shaped, stalked, calcareous Echinoderms.

Crustaceans. Crabs, Lobsters, Shrimps, etc., having a hard shell or crust.

Diatoms. Very minute plants provided with siliceous envelopes.

Dorsal. Connected with the back.

Echinoderms. Starfish, Sea-urchins or Sea-eggs, Holothurians, and Crinoids.

Fathom. Six feet.

Foraminifera. Protozoa having a perforated shell through the holes of which thread-like processes which act as locomotive or feeding organs can be protruded.

Globigerina. Rhizopods with spiny calcareous shells or cases.

Holothurian. A slug or worm-like Echinoderm or Sea Cucumber with a leathery skin.

Hydrocorallinæ. Colonies of zooids secreting a spongy calcareous tissue that contributes largely to the formation of coral reefs.

Hydrozoa. Simple and composite organisms with only one body-cavity.

Horse latitudes. The belt of variable winds and calms between the north limit of the N.E. trades and the " brave west winds."

177 M

Ianthina. A small and delicate pelagic mollusc with a thin blue shell.
Infusoria. Protozoa having a mouth and rudimentary digestive cavity.
Medusæ. Hydrozoa in the form of jelly-fish.
Molluscs. Shell fish.

Noctilucæ. Minute phosphorescent Infusorians.

Ooze. Finely divided bottom deposit.

Palæozoic. Term applied to lowest Fossiliferous strata.
Pectoral fins. Connected with the chest.
Pelagic. Inhabiting the open ocean.
Physalia. A Hydrozoon, called also " Portuguese Man-of-War."
Plankton. Term used for floating organisms that drift with the current.
Polypite. The separate zooid of a Hydrozoon.
Polyzoa. See Bryozoa.
Protozoa. Animals composed of simple protoplasm.
Pteropods. Minute free-swimming molluscs.
Pyrosoma. See Tunicates. They are brilliantly phosphorescent.

Radiolarians. Rhizopods with spiny siliceous shells or cases.
Rhizopods. Protozoa capable of protruding thread-like feet at will.
Rotifera. Minute free-swimming animals propelled by ciliæ.

Salpæ. See Tunicates.
Sea-fans. See Alcyonarians.
Sertularia. Colonies of hydroid zoophytes in appearance like a fir.
Siliceous. Composed of flint.
Siphonophora. Oceanic hydrozoa consisting of several polypites supported by a swimming bladder. Very transparent and delicate.
Soft Corals. See Alcyonarians.
" Sounding." (Of Whales) Descending into the depths.

Terrigenous. Derived from the land.
Tunicates (or Ascidians). Sack-like cartilaginous jellies such as Salpa, either simple or compound.

Urchins. Another name for Echinus or Sea-egg.

Velella. The Sally-Man. One of the Oceanic hydrozoa consisting of a blue translucent disc with a vertical crest above and a single polypite and tentacles below.
Viscous. Not easily separated or parted.
Water-vascular. Circulating water system.

Zooids. Independent organisms produced by gemmation or fission, sometimes attached to one another and sometimes detached.

INDEX

179